Spaces of Uncertainty

Berlin Revisited

Introduction *Kenny Cupers* **A city, broken but therefore open, constituting a field of fragmented and indeterminate spaces that are free to appropriate: that is the Berlin Markus Miessen and I portrayed in the summer of 2001, resulting in the publication *Spaces of Uncertainty* (Wuppertal: Müller + Busmann, 2002). Berlin is a city formed by division, destruction, and neglect as much as by planning and construction. These countervailing processes resulted in an abundance of vacant land and leftover urban space, which we experienced being used for loitering, farming, playing, clubbing, trading, dwelling, hiding, and a plethora of other activities. It seemed to us that Berlin's multitude of histories left open not only the future but also the present, as inhabitants were able to shape its open spaces in ways both more immediate and ephemeral than in most other cities. Recognizing such spaces as an important ground for freedom of individual action and collective desire, our aim was to counter the then dominant narratives of loss, commercialization, and militarization that shaped debates about public space. In the urban**

margins of Berlin we found a vital resource for public life and the city at large.

One of the central assumptions that shaped our thinking in this project was the opposition between space and place. On the one hand, the city can be understood to produce spaces that are fundamentally shaped by a multiplicity of forces and events, and are therefore fluid and full of potential for change. On the other hand, the city can be conceived as a collection of places designed to be stable and defined, and which require money, power, and investment. The stability of place and its controlled development over time presumes an urban image, a project in which architecture plays a central role. What we reacted to as young graduates was exactly this conservative, or at least stabilizing function of architecture. A focus on the fundamental uncertainty of urban space as opposed to the certainty of place required, so we assumed, a resolute emphasis on the present.

In opposition to the historic gaze that fuels Berlin's growing tourist industry as well as the discussions over heritage preservation so central to planning for the future, we saw in Berlin's urban margins the need for an acute presentism. A focus on the here and now would avoid the pitfalls of projection, whether they be from the past or into the future. Acknowledging the power of the margin therefore was a push against the inevitable becoming-history of the city. Not surprisingly then, we were hesitant about the idea to revisit and rephotograph the same sites fifteen years later. Revisiting would mean acknowledging the importance of historical time, the inevitability of urban change, and the power of place. More fundamentally, would it not nullify our central argument, resting on the denial of Berlin's historicity? Would we not be succumbing to the same kind of place-bound nostalgia that we set out to critique in the first place? Or, might, by contrast, hindsight reveal that the documentary project of *Spaces of Uncertainty* was less a "dirty realism," as Hilde Heynen then called it, than a youthful idealism that was anyway untenable? Curiosity won, and as we returned, first casually and then more and more systematically, we saw many vacant spaces filled in and others left untouched. Some sites had become profitable investments while others had remained undeveloped, continuing to exist in a state of prolonged uncertainty. How could one make sense of such change?

The act of revisiting presumes distance. Distance is what allows one to return to a space and experience it anew. But that experience is of course never really new, shot through as it is with personal memories, cultural assumptions, mediated impressions, and urban images both overdetermined and unidentified. The urban thinkers we invited to contribute to this volume all have a different distance to Berlin, which allows them to convey different senses of its urban change. Some of them are long-term experts and residents of Berlin, while others have only just visited the city. Yet they all suggest, in one way or another, that Berlin has shifted away from being a city of vacancies and uncertainty. Whether it is due to the arrival of global neoliberal development or amounts to the belated realization of the post-reunification dream to turn Berlin into a "normal city," as Florian Hertweck suggests, the photographic comparisons in this book can be read as evidence of such a shift. But their reading is not exhausted by a single interpretation, and they convey more than just the filling up of urban voids. They also show how the urban margins become cannibalized in the process of urban development, by aestheticizing exactly those spaces and qualities that are being pushed out. Or, as Miriam Paeslack writes, in the process of reclaiming vacant land, the aesthetics of urban vacancy and neglect are being recuperated and reappear as hyperculture. This is part of a global political economic process, as Mariana Mogilevich points out, in which tactical urbanism—such as self-building, street vending, or urban bricolage—is no longer the weapon of the weak but becomes an instrument to be used by everyone, including especially by powerful corporations and government institutions. In effect, this is a process of controlled, commercial enterprise exploiting the urban margins. This volume demonstrates the contradictory effects of a globalized hipster urbanism, in which maker culture pop-up stores work in tandem with top-down strategies of real estate speculation and large-scale development.

Yet as Margaret Crawford suggests and the photographic comparisons attest, this process of colonization is not a blanket one. Even though political-economic processes manifest themselves in remarkably similar urban aesthetics around the globe, they do not play out indifferent to any city's historical and contemporary specificity. The success of urban development increasingly depends on its ability to feed off of this urban specificity and to reproduce it as a docile image. Yet a city is still deeper than any image. Philipp Misselwitz discusses the example of Tempelhof Airfield to show that government or developers do not always win in Berlin. But as their plans to build housing on the vast site of the old airport-turned-park were rejected by local residents, perhaps neither does the citizenry at large. Even though we can celebrate this as democratic bottom-up decision-making, the rejection can also be understood as a kind of NIMBYism that ultimately does not benefit the city at large, since Berlin lost an opportunity to increase its stock of affordable housing. This is especially crucial to a city with rapidly rising rents and property values, demonstrating that the life of the urban margins is intimately tied to the right to housing. In a half-postsocialist city, with large-scale public land ownership and common-property forms of housing, both vacant land and housing constitute a commons under threat. The spaces of uncertainty then are not just to be found outside, but also and perhaps increasingly, inside the houses and apartment blocks of the city, as Jesko Fezer suggests.

In this context, Berlin's urban image—to which this book contributes—may play a contradictory role. Representations of the urban margin clearly participate in the insidiously cannibalizing process of contemporary urbanism. The image of Berlin as a city of street food stalls and urban beaches has indeed long found its way into the machinery of city branding: Berlin as the poor-but-sexy capital of Europe. It is not only the monuments—from the Wall and the Television Tower to the city palace that is currently under construction—that stand like the

reanimated ghosts of a bygone society, but also its graffitied walls, its vacant overgrown lots, and its postindustrial wasteland. At the same time, as history produces its own uncertainties, this book may leave open the possibility of alternative futures. At least it leaves these questions unanswered: Can we still approach the urban margin as crucial to the public domain in that it harbors the spontaneous and the unexpected? And can we still see in the city an enchanted world that lies beyond the functional, the controlled, the intentional, and the planned?

I.
ESSAYS

“Berlin shows how the identity of a city is not in its architecture but next to it.”

Spaces of Uncertainty *Kenny Cupers and Markus Miessen*

Grounds for Urban Space To think about the identity of a city is to think about the collection of sites and spaces that together signify that city. This is the opposite of identifying the city with big stories, architects, historic characters, or any such clearly identifiable influences. The identities of a city lie in its struggle to administer its everyday activities. At that moment when the institutionalized whole is overruled by the everyday, immediate identities are born.

Berlin demands that one thinks about the unconscious opposition of space and place, of site and project. The latter is produced by the narrative practices in which architecture plays an important role. Architects like to foresee future identity. They rarely seem to look at the present nature of a site, of the city.

A focus on identity requires, in architectural terms, talking about systems of representation. The architectural project is a storytelling practice that produces an image; specifically, an image of the site. Architectural production is based on the self-conscious construction of particular sites. By deconstructing that which exists, architectural vision transforms grounds into sites and sites into objects. Only this transformation describes the becoming of urban ground, the shift from space into place. Alternatively, with Michel de Certeau, *space* can be understood as the bundled velocities and intersections of mobile elements. Like spoken language, *space* is dependent upon its contextual conversation. *Place*, in this scheme, is the order of elements, the force that determines the relationship of coexistence. *Place* excludes the possibility of elements coexisting within the same location; it is the structured organization of elements always situated beside one another. Whereas *place* equals fixity in location and identity, *space* is constituted by a vectorial description of dynamic forces.

This configuration of opposing entities evokes the question of how urban identity is constituted within the immediateness of the city's ground rather than by architecture and its apparent imagery. An architectural plan or project is generally a projection of a site; it is a story about a space that thereby turns it into a place. In contrast, immediate identity is about the sense of the spaces that make up the city, not about all the projections that try to tie its identity down for the sake of a singular story. Immediate identity seems to exist through the temporary use of ill-defined sites. Sites without projects. In this sense, Berlin's identity is merely a shadow of architecture, despite all attempts to construct its identity through architecture and ideological urbanism. Berlin shows how the identity of a city is not in its architecture but next to it. Beside the architecture, we can hear the whispering voice of societies, the memories and predictions differing from one another without categorization. They inhabit the vagueness of every future moment that does not exclude questions but allows for a multiplicity of immediate responses.

Public Space and its Margins Public space—with its mechanisms of control—has an other, situated in the fragility and indefiniteness of certain spaces and activities. Both atmospheres influence us in the way we live, the way we communicate, and the way we think. How ambiguous are our desires, dreams, and projections? Can we today enjoy only the sterile places with clearly defined uses? Will the designer shops, the fancy cafés, or the commercial promenades provide satisfaction? What about the social public spaces in the back of our heads? Do we still consider the possibility of diverse encounters, including with the nonconsumer, to be the other? What about the young, the restless, the old, the poor, and those who have been excluded from contemporary public spaces and therefore removed from society?

Public space and urbanity have always been connected to disorder, functional heterogeneity, and diversity. The most meaningful character of the metropolis lies in this multiplicity beyond physical borders. The urban public sphere can therefore be based on a model of confrontation and instability, as it is characterized by encounters and confrontations between people. Public spaces are—or at least should be—places where the individual and the community can, openly and insecurely, meet. The functional units, the highly structured, programmed, and controlled spaces in the contemporary city mean to threaten the city's crucial characteristics—namely, openness and unpredictability. The margin is an essential aspect of public space conserving all these crucial characteristics, as it is the preferred space of uncertainty in the contemporary city.

The Transitory Other Architects dream to build. Their confident lines on the drawing board signify plans directed toward a bright and shining future.

Traditionally, architects have always stood on the front line of modern society's warfare against the existing. They have been the ones to direct and design the city of tomorrow. The driving force of such encounters is a genuine faith in progress. However, the projections of architects' desires not only describe sensitivity toward society but show a distorted hidden pleasure: The desire to build is supported by the desire for power. In their attempt to sell their subjective dreams for tangible vehicles of progress, architects luxuriate in the power handed to them by society. Legitimizing their social position, though, means hiding this pleasure. Ethics are the means of doing so: Architects understand their power as a positive tool in making the world a better place. Patronizing, ironic, dogmatic, or cynical, the different modes of communicating the ethical message are all directed to support the architect's legitimacy.

The architect, however, fundamentally misconceives this desire. In contrast to the expectation of architects—the illusion that their child made of stone will enhance the lived environment—reality offers no guarantee for a better future. This is partly connected to the specificity of architectural production. Because architecture is bound to focus its energy on a limited location, it always leaves things behind. These leftovers constitute a marginal position, the ultimately transitory attitude that connotes powerlessness or a refusal to intervene in the world. Unlike architectural structures and programs, the margin does not do anything toward a nearby or faraway future. It is simply there.

This margin is the place where architecture reaches the border of intentional intervention. It is the very space in which architects lose their power, where we are confronted with the impossibility of designing an environment. While the negative aspects of the margin show architecture's limits, its positive characteristics prove the redundancy of the architect. We do not seem to need architects to create our own markets, meeting places, or parties. Playgrounds are preferably not defined by them. Such spaces are best when naturally molded around the action taking place.

This is the humility with which we have tried to approach architecture. It could be categorized as a useless approach for the profession. Nothing about it necessarily points to the putting of theory into practice. However, tracing these spaces can help us understand how the built environment functions.

The margin strongly demystifies often used terms such as *development* and *process*. Traditionally, architecture is involved with the development of empty sites into well-defined developed places. This is supposed to constitute the continual process of developing a city. Nobody will claim this process has an endpoint. There is no final product, no perfect city. The city is a never-ending cycle of growth and decay. The architectural project is fully developed in its design phase; once built it is immovable. As a result, the city consists of frozen moments of solid architecture. Architecture's sloth seems bound to freeze the city's dynamism.

The margin—as the immediate stage of architecture's side effects—offers a second perspective to the specific nature of architectural production. In opposition to architecture, the space of the margin allows for a more direct idea of process, a continual one. The physical leftover is a ground of ephemeral traces and offers simultaneity of difference, qualities that the places of architectural development are lacking in their exclusiveness. The margin thus functions as a delayed catalyst of urban culture. Architecture's instrumental nature enables us to understand the margin as a local recollection of the other, a memorial testimony of tactical space. Occupied by whispering narratives rather than visual representation, this continuity in space and time is an enormous resource, perhaps the ultimate buffer zone in the contemporary city.

The margin evokes an architectural understanding which lies far beyond its own discipline. The question remains, however, of how to deal with the ever-present desire of implementation. The practice of annihilation tends to support and satisfy the desire to fill up the in-between, to diminish its possibilities, to replace uncertainty with definition. If we, in the end, are to make up a final balance, this is the goal that has directed our energy: An increased sensitivity (on the part of professionals involved in our urban environments) toward the hidden possibilities that lie within the margin and its practice. And although the step from this marginal urban research into consistent design practice is far from self-evident, the underlying motives can instigate thinking about a different urban practice: one of a realistic understanding of the existing, toward a more open and potent future.

The existence of these spaces of uncertainty is both a relief and a promise. While breathing our eternal desire for a humane homecoming on inhumane territory, it is as undefined as we are. In our attempt to structure the chaos that space initially is, the margins have become the last reminder of who we are. They are inhabited by the other and inhabit the oppositions, from which our phony worlds are put together.

Extract of the publication ***Spaces of Uncertainty***, ed. Kenny Cupers and Markus Miessen (Wuppertal: Müller + Busmann, 2002).

“Faced with the evidence of urban change it is human nature to impose narratives. No matter how partial or contradictory our information, it is almost impossible to avoid reading change as directional, demonstrating progress or decay and, psychologically most important, good or bad.”

Making Sense of Change *Margaret Crawford* Revisiting the sites of *Spaces of Uncertainty* underlines a fundamental fact of urbanism: change. Cities are never static, but constantly transform themselves. Some grow, others shrink. Cities expand upward and grow outward or deteriorate and empty out. Sometimes both processes occur as centers migrate to new locations, and neighborhoods lose their functions. New populations arrive, relocate, and depart. Enormous enterprises of finance, development, planning, regulation, and design exist to manage these processes, but rarely are able to fully control or direct them.

Faced with the evidence of urban change it is human nature to impose narratives. No matter how partial or contradictory our information, it is almost impossible to avoid reading change as directional, demonstrating progress or decay and, psychologically most important, good or bad. As Marshall Berman famously pointed out, urban transformation poses a powerful challenge to our consciousness, pushing us away from its contradictions toward rational explanation.

To someone unfamiliar with Berlin, like myself, these images raise more questions than they answer. But even without any contextual information, it is tempting to speculate about the meanings visible in these paired images. The most immediate narrative visible is one linked to political economy, explaining Berlin's changes as one iteration of globalization. This describes a pattern of rampant neoliberalization, development driven by real estate and foreign investment, and based on new city images connected to global models of urbanization. New malls, well-designed modern apartments, and sidewalk cafés have replaced empty lots and neglected infrastructure. There are more cars, more fences and less graffiti, all of which might be seen as evidence of the city's restructuring according to the dictates of capital. Local needs and priorities, especially of the less affluent, are ignored in the race to attract investment and wealthier residents. Many observers would read these changes as a narrative of loss, documenting the disappearance of a poorer, emptier, but more distinctive city.

But a closer look complicates this story. A surprising number of the empty spaces depicted in the first book are still there. Greener and overgrown, they suggest that urban nature has its own temporalities. In part, their persistence demonstrates the erratic pace of urban change, full of gaps and delays. But it also suggests that even neoliberal processes of development are patchy and incomplete rather than totalizing, adding just another layer to the city's strata. Other changes seem to be genuine civic improvements, such as the simple park that has replaced the junked car and muddy field as a place for children to play.

Another surprise is the number of people visible in the later images. Is this accidental, or do they represent population growth, the new inhabitants who will live and work in the buildings under construction? If these residents have fewer opportunities for making their own spaces, they seem to have many more public spaces being made for them. They can spend time pleasantly in the dedicated quasi-public spaces of the malls, sidewalk cafés, or beer gardens. Their presence suggests another narrative, that of progress and improvement, of action and movement rather than the stillness that the earlier spaces convey. Proponents of "placemaking" discourses such as Jan Gehl, who measure the success of public spaces by the numbers of people they attract, would see these changes as positive. But these messy, functional spaces are still very far from Gehl's model for ideal pedestrian piazzas.

One limit of such public spaces is their certainty. Deck chairs neatly lined up facing the sun define only a single option rather than the infinite number of possibilities that the empty spaces suggest. But even these limited uses are still temporary. Perhaps, since none of the chairs appears to be occupied, they will disappear soon, replaced by other, more appealing options. The mall may appear to be more permanent, but as Americans have discovered, even monumental shopping centers have limited lives.

Why do we feel the need to impose clear narratives on urban changes that are anything but clear? Perhaps because they make sense of the past and point to knowable futures. Identifying changes as trajectories imposes an order that probably does not exist. It is difficult to accept ambiguity and uncertainty. As historians we want time to have significance. But projecting the present into the future is a mistake. Berlin, like every important city, has produced many imagined and planned futures that never happened.

As individuals we respond to urban changes with mixed emotions, lamenting the loss of familiar places and activities while welcoming those that fit our own preferences. Only those most driven by ideology can ignore their own ambivalence. Each of the two Berlins pictured here appeals in different ways. The riverside beer garden looks like a more comfortable place to spend a few hours than its sandy predecessor. During the winter, the mall will offer refuge from the cold that renders the empty lots uninhabitable. But it is hard not to mourn the passing of the empty spaces. They played an important role in the city by keeping spatial and social possibilities alive. Both before and after, they projected an ambiguous temporality, no longer but not yet. Their uncertainty undermined the assurance of new development. Deserted green spaces next to sleek offices defamiliarized the city, their untended emptiness questioning the permanence of glass and steel and reminding us of previous Berlins. And most important, the unexpected presence of a horse in a landscape of skyscrapers suggested that urban magic was still a possibility.

“Berlin, with its polycentric orientation of different mixed neighborhoods, is increasingly becoming socially transformed into a pyramidally structured city with a golden center for the few in which the original alternative scene is now misused as an advertising aspect.”

Eldorado Berlin *Florian Hertweck* In the mid-1990s I visited a city for the first time that was completely different from Paris, where I had made my home. Apart from the more prestigious areas, which were also somewhat bizarre in their own way, Berlin's central districts looked exactly like the photos in this book: seemingly endless expanses where nature was left to run wild or everything was covered by concrete slabs between which weeds proliferated, here and there warehouses, snack stalls and kiosks, while the firewalls of destroyed block structures and serially produced housing complexes with their best days well behind them towered in the background. Everything seemed the opposite of Paris, probably the most planned of all planned metropolises, like a haphazard piece of suburbia uninformed by even the most basic concept of cohesive urban spaces or town-planning compositional schemata, a fluid urban space that seemed to be readily accessible.

In contrast to the experience of the generic suburb, walking or cycling through these unfinished spaces proved extremely exciting, above all because of their aura. The firewalls and bullet holes visible everywhere on the semi-derelict facades, the footprints of historical urban squares, and the obsolete infrastructures provided a sense of what a crystallization point this city had once been, a city in which, as Paul Virilio put it, "a pitiless century was reflected."[1] In contrast to the "Capital of the Nineteenth Century" it was not the built environment, not the heroic monuments or historical urban structures that rendered history experienceable, but rather that which was no longer there. Berlin was a city where "something was lacking," as Cees Nooteboom put it in his *Berliner Notizen*.[2] It was a city of the "bombed away" and the "mysteriously forbidden" in which the "connections of history" had to be read "from its very fissures," in the formulation of Wim Wenders, who had also returned to the city because he found it able to narrate its historicity more arrestingly through its scarred cityscape than "any history book or [historical] document."[3]

Unlike Paris, Berlin at the time could also not be experienced or treated in terms of classical aesthetic categories; it evoked other ideas of city and other types of use. The spaces of this *city without form*, as Philipp Oswalt so aptly termed it, were not spaces of uncertainty in the sense that one felt threatened there, but in terms of their ownership status.[4] Many of the propertics appropriated by the GDR were returned to their rightful owners, who in turn often sold them, with the result that these properties became the object of feasibility studies and planning projects. At the same time the city (still) owned much more real estate than it was capable of developing. As a result this land could be freely utilized by third parties. In fine weather, for instance, a few barrows of sand would be dumped somewhere and deck chairs set up. Parties were held on vacant lots and then moved on after a time to other unused locations. People of my age moved into dilapidated apartments that were empty and whose ownership status was unclear. Everything was possible, and everything could end very soon.

Cloud-Cuckoo-Land In the mid-1990s the development of Berlin entered a phase in which the controversy over reconstruction slowly died down. The most prominent properties had been sold, the most important competitions run, and Hans Stimmann, Berlin's building director, had implemented his idiosyncratic interpretation of critical reconstruction in the face of significant resistance, an interpretation which rejected the inclusion of social housing in a more or less critical reconstruction of the historical layout of the city, as foreseen by the International Building Exhibition (1984–87), and instead proposed to cast the new, mostly tertiary structures into historical (or as on Potsdamer Platz, historicizing) streetscapes and squares from the prewar period in order to liberate the inner city—a concept that had not played any role in the prior history of Berlin—from its supposedly abnormal, depleted, and dual existence. According to the self-described rationalists around Stimmann, Berlin was to be architecturally and urbanistically normalized, that is, transformed into what they understood as a normal European metropolis. Although at this time the euphoria of reunification had not completely evaporated, it was no longer as intense as it had been in the years directly following the fall of the Wall—when the city was regarded as an Eldorado for investors who, fired up by tax breaks, seized on the idea that the new capital would soon be in the same league as Paris and London, when firms like Daimler-Benz, whose core business had nothing to do with real estate economics, were electrified by prognoses that Berlin's population was going to increase to five million by the end of the millennium and that the city would need more than 800,000 dwellings by 2010 as well as 22.5 million square meters of floor space for commerce and industry. The aim, as Hans Stimmann wrote in the journal *Bauwelt* in 1991, was "to develop Berlin as a modern city, the German capital and the venue for the 2000 Olympic Games."[5]

"In the years after 1989 it was like living in cloud-cuckoo-land [in Berlin]," stated Thilo Sarrazin in a remarkable interview twenty years after the fall of the Wall. "Everyone was talking about the 'hub between East and West' but nothing substantial happened. Industry collapsed in eastern Berlin, and it collapsed in western Berlin. [...] Berlin grew [economically] up until 1997 slightly more than the German average. Today we know that this was because of the construction boom. At some point the Berlin building-tycoon cartel collapsed and prices normalized. [...] Today the Berlin construction industry is rightly in pieces and has to rebuild itself. [...] The extraordinary phenomenon of an extremely large amount of public money being pumped into a few square kilometers was regarded as normal. [...] It was just one mistake after another! And afterward Berlin underwent a period of shrinkage therapy."[6]

After the population began to decline again in the mid-1990s and, contrary to the expectations of the city's political decision-makers, the large-scale relocation to Berlin of leading business enterprises failed to materialize, and after the dismal failure of the bid in 1993 for the 2000 Olympic Games, which had been considered a sure thing, few people believed Berlin's mayor at the time, Eberhard Diepgen, when in 1996 he promised his city a leading economic role in Europe.[7] Gradually doubts began to be voiced regarding Berlin's development into a metropolis and the ambitious Berlin 2000 project, which was obviously no longer able to generate the effect of a self-fulfilling prophecy. Witness to the megalomania of these years is Berlin's Hauptbahnhof, the city's central railway station, which was planned for a far larger population and stood stranded for years, like Hans Hollein's aircraft carrier, in the Berlin steppe north of the Federal Chancellery.

Antieconomy The positive side of this economic hangover during the second half of the 1990s was that the high degree of mixed use could be maintained. The examples of available spaces referred to above had flourished to such an extent precisely because of the fact that cranes were swinging over the capital and every protagonist assumed that the unfinished, open city would very quickly be transformed into a finished, cohesive city. Since this transformation was now unachievable in the foreseeable future, the counterculture could approach the whole issue in a more relaxed fashion. As a result the late 1990s and early 2000s were, according to Diedrich Diederichsen, still decidedly "antieconomic": "No one wanted to be developed, and not a lot was developed. The dominant mentality was to be as unproductive as possible, to accomplish as little as possible if one wanted to maintain this situation."[8]

In temporarily used spaces the situation still seemed akin to that seen on the opening night of the legendary Cookies club: "We spent the whole day in panic trying to get everything together we needed for a bar," said the initiator, Heinz Gindullis. "When we opened and the first guests were arriving, there weren't even any drinks on the bar."[9]

In the Berlin of the 1990s the development of land supported by public monies was thus confronted by a refusal to develop anything or be developed oneself. These antagonistic attitudes toward the city, both of which could draw on models from Berlin's history, formed the basis of the allure of Berlin, which was increasingly mythologized both nationally and internationally.

Paradigm Shift At the beginning of the 2000s the wind seemed to have gone well and truly out of the sails of supporters of development. The so-called Berlin bank scandal in 2001 not only brought to light machinations in business and politics for which West Berlin was infamous; the impenetrable construct that had been established misappropriated public monies on a previously barely conceivable scale, which was to have a lasting impact on the city's budget. It is an irony of Berlin's very particular history that, after the Berlin banking scandal had cost the mayor, Eberhard Diepgen, and finance senator, Klaus-Rüdiger Landowsky, their jobs, a Berlin government made up of Social Democrats and members of the Left party set out to clean up the finances of a city whose unemployment rate would rise to a whopping 18 percent by 2006. "Save till it squeals," was the motto of the new mayor, Klaus Wowereit, whose finance senator, Thilo Sarrazin, felt compelled to devise a menu for welfare recipients made up of bratwurst and sauerkraut, with which he wanted to prove that a single-person-household could manage with just under four euros a day, thereby obviating the need for any increase in state aid. Seven years before the Europe-wide financial and euro crisis, the German capital found itself subject to a program of austerity devised by a left-wing government that extended to the lowest level of the socioeconomic spectrum.

The effect of this apocalyptic mood in the field of urban policy led to the development of new approaches. Three years after the banking scandal the public was presented with an urban-development concept for the year 2020, the austere character of which was officially emphasized and which postulated a total departure from the previous strategy. "Realism is what is needed," was the central statement of this concept. "In view of the city's empty coffers, strategic planning and action to promote sustainable urban development will no longer be determined by the steering and distribution of growth. The emphasis must be on current Berliners making use of opportunities." Berlin, stated the authors from the Senate Administration for Urban Development, had "the image of a city in upheaval." The official stance now was that the city was unfinished and as a result was open to new things, which led to the following conclusion: "[This image] is an important factor in attracting young and creative people to Berlin. The breadth of cultural offerings, ranging from traditional to alternative, is making a significant contribution to the attractiveness of the city. The cultural sector has generated a production network that has a direct effect on, for instance, tourism and the development of the retail sector. Developing the economic effects of culture and optimizing them with the targeted use of public funds will be enormously significant for long-term urban development."[10]

Clearly, with their options severely limited, city policymakers had recognized the economic potential of the very cultural scene that had originally not wanted to be developed. Suddenly the heterogeneous character of Berlin and the countercultural scene were no longer comprehended as the enemy of an urban development based on stone facades, but instead a magnet that could attract people—preferably young and creative—as new residents or tourists to the city in the longer term. The phenomenon of multisided temporary use, which had previously met with, at best, patronizing smiles, was now used to promote the city. One campaign was titled "Berlin has been through a lot. Every weekend," while another postulated "Elsewhere prices are exploding, but in Berlin it's the mood that's sky-high." Whereas the official diction of Berlin in the 1990s had been that of a normalized metropolis, the attitude opposing this diction now became a fundamental element of the political discourse. Being Berlin, according to the credo of the 36.5-million-euro campaign "Be Berlin" now meant: "Be open, be free, be Berlin." No one gave better expression to this paradigm shift than the then mayor Klaus Wowereit with his legendary phrase: "Berlin is poor but sexy."

Asset Development Following the crisis years Berlin actually did become a kind of Eldorado for an increasing number of people who were looking for the opportunity not to turn cement into gold but to unapologetically self-actualize—hedonists from other major European cities and, increasingly, former residents of southwestern Germany deprecatingly referred to as "Prenzlschwaben" and "Mitte-Franken," i.e., Swabians and Franconians, who bought property in the trendy Berlin suburbs of Prenzlauer Berg and Mitte. These were people who had access to money, through inheritance or otherwise, and were attracted by the extremely low cost of living in Berlin and its very particular easiness. "Earlier, when I visited Berlin as a tourist, I was envious when I saw so many young people sitting in cafés at lunchtime with their laptops and apparently having a great time," a young Parisian told us when we were working on the book *Dialogic City*. "The relaxed pace of life in Berlin so appealed to me that I gave up my stressful job in Paris and moved here, where I also became part of this easygoing crowd who spent their days in cafés. However, after a few months I began to feel a sense of inertia. I became depressed and had to move back to Paris and my old job."

At the same time members of the alternative scene began to cash in on their pioneering ideas. The idea of setting up a few deck chairs on some sand evolved into organized beach bars. The kind of concept represented by Cookies in its initial manifestation was taken up and applied to professional restaurants and bars. The constant shifting of party locations ended to the same degree as the income of their initiators stabilized. The rough-and-ready was now increasingly staged, from within and from without—improvisation was in. Urban development was now—per force—no longer understood as classical planning but as the making possible or formalization of types of utilization that had initially developed in an uncontrolled and informal manner.

A new field opened up for many architects who had been starved of work over many years. Those of us who had worked in France were accustomed to being constantly confronted with the dogma of master planning, and so when we took part in an open ideas competition for the development of the northern area of Tempelhof Airport, which had just been closed, we found the concept of an explicitly process-oriented urban development extremely exciting. How could architects approach a situation involving the development of a gigantic, publicly owned area which was scheduled to be sold because the city no longer saw itself as having the means to guarantee the maintenance and illumination of the undeveloped areas, while at the same time potential buyers or developers were nowhere in sight because there was simply no demand for such a project? Certainly not with classical town planning. Architects were now faced with the challenge of walking a tightrope between generating processes and activities and avoiding the freezing of these processes through formalization. And this relatively new architectural approach gradually developed into a new economy.

Homogenization In retrospect it would seem that Wowereit's strategy was in fact successful. The staging of activities and spaces that were still open, free, decidedly antieconomic, and in some cases subversive in the 1990s led to a new demographic growth, booming mass tourism, the emergence of new economic sectors, and ultimately to a new wave of development of city real estate. In the meantime, the third and fourth generations of new residents have arrived in the city, groups that often bring considerable financial means and are populating the so-called inner city, while mass tourism—for the most part the low-cost tourism of the easyJet set—is furthering the growth of backpacker hostels. At the same time an increasing number of enterprises are moving to Berlin, which is styling itself as a hotspot of digitization. In the meantime "half of the companies in the city are showing what digitization looks like."[11] It seems that Richard Florida's concept of the creative class, which posits that companies locate themselves where they can find qualified employees (rather than the opposite) is being realized in Berlin, which is exactly where these potential employees want to live. Finally—and this is a consequence of this new development—Berlin real estate is now being subjected to a new and powerful wave of asset development which is no longer being publicly financed or organized but instead left to the free market. "The building industry is moving in here in spectacular dimensions," says

Dieter Hoffmann-Axthelm. "You can see this in the area around the Hauptbahnhof and in many other parts of the city. Huge chunks of stone are being deposited. It's the second 'clumping' of the city, the first being the same phenomenon we saw along Friedrichstrasse during the 1990s. This is incredibly damaging for the city because this enormous investment doesn't for a second take account of the possible presence of more middle-income people." Hoffmann-Axthelm, the author of *Die Dritte Stadt* (The Third City), sees this as a result of the Berlin government's complete withdrawal from the debate around the development of the city[12] and the haphazard sale of city property, half of which was publicly owned following the fall of the Wall and the best parts of which, as Tim Renner puts it, were "converted into cash by Sarrazin."[13] In the last five years massive real estate speculation in Berlin has raised prices by almost 44 percent and the base rental index by 10 percent. In central locations real estate developers are now aiming for prices comparable to other major European cities such as Paris.

To this extent, Hans Stimmann's concept of a normalized and homogenized capital has been realized but in a different way than originally envisaged. Although the city's central areas are not particularly homogeneous in architectural terms, they certainly meet this criterion in social and economic terms. The unique social mix in these districts has made way for a population structure that embodies more or less the same lifestyle. Berlin, with its polycentric orientation of different mixed neighborhoods, is increasingly becoming socially transformed into a pyramidally structured city with a golden center for the few in which the original alternative scene is now misused as an advertising aspect. Niklas Maak refers to this as the zombification of the city: "The new luxury building projects [such as Yoo and Kronprinzengärten] are not only bringing about good old gentrification by supplanting the simple and provisional with a more prosperous middle-class lifestyle. They are zombifying the city: They are resurrecting what they are supplanting—the studios, the small art spaces, the improvised, the provisional—as a value-enhancing, invigorating image." The new city, sums up Maak, is copying "as a fiction what it has just supplanted: The artist is supposed to lend the commercially harmonized new luxury quarter the aroma of urban resistance. He is permitted to return to the site of his supplantation to conceal from the residents the sterility that comes with them."[14]

An interesting duel can thus be observed over the period since the fall of the Wall: between the economic development of the city and the antieconomic alternative scene, which at the beginning of the new century seemed to be on the rise, when Berlin was the site of a postgrowth society—as witnessed by the photos in this book. But ultimately it is capitalism that has emerged from this duel as the victor, because it has not only been able to develop the antieconomic as an asset but has even been able to instrumentalize it as a means of promotion.

1 Paul Virilio, *L'espace critique* (Paris: C. Bourgois, 1984), 148.
2 Cees Nooteboom, *Berliner Notizen* (Frankfurt a.M.: Suhrkamp, 1991), 40.
3 Wim Wenders, "The Urban Landscape," in Wim Wenders, *The Act of Seeing: Essays and Conversation* (London: Faber & Faber, 1997), 123.
4 Philipp Oswalt, *Berlin: Stadt ohne Form: Strategien einer anderen Architektur* (Munich: Prestel, 2000).
5 Hans Stimmann, "Berliner Abkommen," *Bauwelt*, special edition (1991): 2002.
6 Thilo Sarrazin, "Klasse statt Masse: Von der Hauptstadt der Transferleistungen zur Metropole der Eliten: Thilo Sarrazin im Gespräch," *Lettre International*, no. 86 (2009): 197.
7 Eberhard Diepgen, foreword to *Berlin: En bref* (Berlin: Presse- und Informationsamt des Landes Berlin, 1996), 1.
8 "Du willst doch nicht an einen Ort gehen, der für dich gemacht ist. Diedrich Diederichsen und Tim Renner im Gespräch mit Arno Brandlhuber und Florian Hertweck," in *Dialogic City: Berlin wird Berlin*, ed. Arno Brandlhuber, Florian Hertweck, and Thomas Mayfried (Cologne: Walther König, 2015), 383.
9 Annika Schönstädt, "Das 'Cookies' ist Geschichte," *Die Welt*, July 21, 2014.
10 Senatsverwaltung für Stadtentwicklung, *Stadtentwicklungskonzept 2020: Statusbericht und perspektivische Handlungsansätze* (Berlin: Kulturbuch-Verlag, 2004), 3-4.
11 Joachim Fahrun, "Neue Firmen schaffen Tausende Jobs in Berlin: Berlin wird attraktiver: Die Wirtschaftsförderer von Berlin Partner verzeichnen 2015 60 Prozent mehr Ansiedelungen als im Vorjahr," *Berliner Morgenpost*, December 26, 2015.
12 Dieter Hoffmann-Axthelm, unpublished transcript of a lecture given within the framework of a debate on Berlin organized by Arno Brandlhuber and Florian Hertweck in Krampnitz on June 14, 2014. Archive of Florian Hertweck.
13 "Du willst doch nicht an einen Ort gehen, der für dich gemacht ist: Diedrich Diederichsen und Tim Renner im Gespräch mit Arno Brandlhuber und Florian Hertweck," in *Dialogic City*, 393 (see note 8).
14 Niklas Maak, "Die Wohnfrage: Aussichten für eine zombiefizierte Stadt," in *Dialogic City*, 465 (see note 8).

“The late twentieth century’s life processes of acceleration and absorption by technology are being given a reprieve of sorts by using photography. Post-Wall Berlin is given to an aesthetics of both disappearance and reappearance, set in motion by the city’s division and reunification.”

Aesthetics of Reappearance *Miriam Paeslack*

> *"Reality is produced by a society's culture, it is not given.*
> *A reality that has been produced by one society will be taken over,*
> *and changed by another, younger society, producing fresh reality.*
> *This happens first by mimicry, then by substitution, and the*
> *original reality will, by that time, be totally forgotten."*[1]

A pair of urban landscape photographs clearly captured from the same spot present a kind of riddle. Which one was taken first? Both feature the easily recognizable Berlin Television Tower vertically marking the image's golden ratio on the left. On the right, we recognize in each image the modernist tower of the former Hotel Berlin, now the Park Inn by Radisson Hotel. Both images resist being set in time, their respective messiness suggesting random stages of demolition or growth. Despite some detectable compositional sensibility, the witness of these two instances appears to be a rather casual flâneur. In this and other diptychs in this series, the alignment of two viewpoints is only approximate. We see urban objects such as concrete paving, a neglected piece of lawn, a car, a street food stall, a midsize tree in one image and a graffiti-tagged temporary construction container, several parked cars, a communally operated beer trolley, and the pale pink facade of the Alexa shopping mall at Alexanderplatz in the other (plate 4 page 98). The first image is smaller than the other and framed by a white border, while the second one bleeds across the entire page. This editorial decision inspires questions of how to read the pair and whether to prioritize the larger image while understanding the smaller one as a kind of picture postcard referencing its larger pendant.

These photos are part of a series of such pairs that were photographed fifteen years apart from one another, in 2001 and 2016, to record ephemeral sites in post-reunification Berlin. Spaces of uncertain use and determination emerged and were left thanks to a shifting politics and culture in a reuniting city. Focusing on the desolate, empty, and discontinuous in Berlin's urban and architectural fabric, these images capture sites that triggered both nostalgia and a sense of potential as spaces of opportunity and experimentation. In the span of fifteen years, we see the "voids of Berlin," as Andreas Huyssen called them in the 1990s, transformed, filled, haphazardly touched up, or seemingly returned to another phase of neglect.[2] The original sites of uncertainty, many of which are located near the former site of the Berlin Wall, have at times been turned into profitable investments in a city that has seen real estate prices surge with an enormous influx of young creative urbanites and refugees. But more often than not, these sites are still unresolved, their layout and use still undetermined or undeveloped. Indeed, their transformation process is remarkably subtle and slow, and starkly contrasts with neoliberal narratives of efficient, linear, and progressive development. Despite corporatized visions for Berlin's real estate after 1989, these photographs reveal hesitation, perpetuated uncertainty rather than affirmation and closure.

What are the various conditions for these processes of prolonged uncertainty, and how do photographs create meaning and construct a city? How do temporality, commemoration, and the concept of the urban void figure into these photographs' narratives, and how do they make the city reappear? Discussing his concept of the "aesthetics of disappearance," Paul Virilio explains that in pre-photographic times, "the image had appeared, as it were, through the medium of the canvas. [...] Persistence had a material basis." This changed once persistence became a cognitive rather than material phenomenon with the advent of the photographic sequence and eventually of film. Things "are there, they appear, and are in motion, *because* they vanish afterwards."[3] The photo pairs presented here disrupt this process that Virilio found to characterize late modernity through a catastrophic perception of technology.[4] The late twentieth century's life processes of acceleration and absorption by technology, which deterritorialize us, are being given a reprieve of sorts by using photography. Post-Wall Berlin is given to an aesthetics of both disappearance and reappearance, set in motion by the city's division and reunification.

Void In a classic yet rare before-and-after confrontation, one diptych captures a central Berlin site that shows busy construction (plate 15 page 120): in one image, the site is being readied by fencing off a grassy terrain that still houses a mobile street food stall and is overgrown with bushes. An early twentieth-century building in the middle ground to the left is the oldest structure in the picture. Behind it in the distant background, the residential high-rises of the Fischerinsel help us locate this site on the border between

Mitte and Kreuzberg. Randomly parked cars and scattered concrete barriers in the foreground contrast with indicators of imminent action, two bright red cranes in the middle ground. Quite a lot happened in this site when it was revisited: the historic building is now framed by two mixed-use developments. The cranes seem to have migrated to a site further east, and the grassy lot that was an open wasteland in one image is here fenced off with an orange-brown wooden paneled fence, probably to be developed and transformed into a new building block. Neither site is populated, though each is staged with a subtly clouded blue summer sky.

There is a dynamic in this pair that is at once exciting and anxious. An urban void is being successively filled, emptied, and refilled. The images invoke modernist urban sociological assessments of the city as a place of both spatial and mental growth and tremendous challenges. Sociologist Georg Simmel's student Siegfried Kracauer put this aptly in a text for the *Frankfurter Zeitung* in 1930,

> *Every typical space is generated by typical societal conditions, which articulate themselves in this space without the obstructing interference of consciousness. Everything that is otherwise simply denied by consciousness is part of its construction. Such spatial images are the dreams of society. Wherever we decipher a spatial image's hieroglyphs, we are presented with the foundation of social reality.*[5]

The social reality that these images reveal is one of promise and uncertainty. Creating such spatial images and deciphering them is nothing new in Berlin. Indeed, this species of material before-and-after documentation is part of the representational canon of urban transformation since the Renaissance. In the late nineteenth century, Berlin's unprecedented reshaping into the capital of the German Empire triggered enthusiastic photographic responses in the form of commissioned and self-initiated documentations of destruction and growth. Georg Bartels' paired photos of the demolition and new construction on the corner of Rosenstrasse in Berlin's central Mitte district [1+2] (photographed 1894 and 1896 respectively) bear a striking resemblance to the contemporary ones, as they both seem fascinated by the urban processes of

[1]

[2]

voiding and spatial reclamation. The most obvious differences are Bartels' use of midsize contact collodion prints, which resemble today's digital sepia filters in tone; and his elevated standpoint, which was a common choice, when possible, to present the entirety of a site's change.[6] Bartels' process was laborious, as he had to set up, mount, and move heavy equipment: a tripod, the glass negative plates, and the wooden camera box. Today's photographer, by contrast, spent seconds to identify and capture his images.

Berlin's biography as the capital of the German Empire and of a reunited Germany, both determined by a breathtaking and overwhelming succession of destruction, reconstruction, division, and reunification, lends itself particularly well to narratives of progress and defeat, and reflections of the historical and evolving city. Such characteristics also situate Berlin squarely in familiar debates of a city's place in the history of modernity and what followed. In his 1910 book *Berlin, ein Stadtschicksal*, the critic Karl Scheffler characterized Berlin as being "condemned forever to becoming and never to being." In the same year, cultural critic Max Osborn must have had this sentiment of "never being" in mind when he wrote in the daily *Der Tag* about the contradictions and antagonisms in Berlin's reputation:

> *It is clear now that in front of our eyes a true metropolis emerges out of a far-too-fast-growing community, which sweats of parvenu-ism and the eagerness to show off. From this chaos, we realize now, rises a modern life of character, unfolds from cluelessness a coherent organism.*[7]

Such cluelessness, however, seems to have remained Berlin's modus operandi. Other, even more blunt examples for a site's change and for a void's being filled can be found in diptychs such as number 18 (page 126), where an inner-city wasteland, which was used as an impromptu family hangout and tanning spot in 2001, was populated with seven-story multifamily housing by 2016. A wooden temporary construction site fence, stacked pallets, and bright orange construction containers marking the image's horizon line were telling clues for imminent construction in 2001. Their contrast with the organic shapes and hues of the green of shrubbery and fast-growing trees contributes

[3]

to a dynamic composition. The family of four or five in the picture's middle ground that sat down on the thin grass and parked a stroller nearby seemed unbothered by that equipment in the background. We are looking at a kind of *Déjeuner sur l'herbe* [3] in a significantly modified and sober setting compared with its Parisian precursor. The 2016 photo, however, could almost pass for a developer-commissioned image if not for its lack of context and visible onset of the new inhabitants' individualizations of apartment balconies and window decorations.

Two even bolder examples for the development of a formerly deserted site are diptychs 22 and 23 (page 134/136). Both sets show buildings and their urban setting in the first iteration and the abstractions of retail or office space facades that were erected on these sites in the second one. The image of the famed Tresor (German for "vault") techno club site at Leipziger Strasse resembles an exurban fairground site and features a tent structure in the background on the left of the small cubic and nondescript Tresor facade. The club, which was founded in 1991 and closed in 2005, reappropriated a structure of Berlin's imperial era as it occupied the underground vaults of the former Wertheim department store (built by Alfred Messel and opened in 1896) on Leipziger Platz. The rigid rectangularity of the corporate golden facade and industrial sunshades of the new office building that replaced the club both echo its compact geometry and emphasize and starkly contrast with this institution's transitory and spontaneous character. We get a glimpse of Berlin's evolution from a playground for spontaneous reclamation, squatting, and creative occupations during the 1990s and early 2000s, to the site of corporate development and globalized urban branding. These central parts of Berlin, Leipziger Platz and Potsdamer Platz, were among the first to be systematically developed, as diptych 23 (page 136) makes very clear. By 2001, the no-man's-land, a broad strip for security between what was effectively two walls, had already been planned and built out on the site of Potsdamer Platz. In the 2001 image we see in the background the tent-like silhouette of Sony Center and some of the first buildings that were erected on Leipziger Platz (one of which is the Mosse Center) as well as four of the omnipresent cranes of the millennial Berlin skyline. Berlin at that time invited visitors to this site as "Schaustelle," a portmanteau of the words for *construction site* and *showplace* or *spectacle*. This kind of pumped-up critical reconstruction, as Berlin's building director Hans Stimmann called it, grew both literally and metaphorically on the drawing board, on the tabula rasa of the Wall, which dominates the foreground and lower half of the 2001 image. The outcome was the Mall of Berlin, the facade of which we are staring at in the 2016 image.

Memory While Berlin's voids are often actual material, spatial emptiness, its frequent characterization as a palimpsest refers equally to its mental, mnemonic fracturing.[8] Berlin is a city of layers that are formed by wartime destruction, its division, and phases of demolition and construction, as well as by the absence and memory of its victims of the Holocaust and of the city's wall.[9] Artists such as Christian Boltanski [4][10], Shimon Attie [5][11], and Micha Ullman[12] engaged with that mnemonic void in the city with temporary or lasting interventions during the 1990s and early 2000s. Some of this volume's diptychs too are temporarily extended reflections on the significance and memory of site. They demark some of Berlin's many *lieux de mémoire* without much ado.

[4]

[5]

It is easy to miss the significance of the unassuming metal-clad structure titled "Tränenpalast" (Palace of Tears) that was captured from across the street in diptych 9 (page 108). The composition emphasizes the coincidental nature of its coming into existence. Going up on Friedrichstrasse just past the S and U Bahnhof Friedrichstrasse, the photographer didn't even have to cross the street to engage with this building. Its modesty defies its tremendous significance for travelers across the Iron Curtain just over a decade earlier. This utterly cryptic image presents an East–West checkpoint, shielded from the eyes of passers-by and already branded by spelling out the self-deprecating and sarcastic nickname that Berliners had assigned to this building, Tränenpalast. Fifteen years later, the photographer has halted his city *parcours* (most likely cycling) at seemingly the same spot. The now exposed Palace of Tears starkly contrasts in dimensions with a high-rise office building that has been erected next to it along Friedrichstrasse and that dominates the entire upper right third of the image. What was obscured behind a protective cladding earlier is now revealed, but turns out to be at risk of being overlooked and forgotten due to its small dimensions and fragile frame. The irony of history adds to this particular site another mnemonic dimension. The large, nondescript office tower that overpowers the modest and refrained memorial to Germany's division was built on the site of Mies van der Rohe's 1921/22 design for a lofty glass and steel skyscraper [6] [13]. This building, even though it was never erected, became an icon of modernist architecture while the building on its site was criticized as a lost opportunity and a misled compromise between a daring vision and Berlin's post-Wall reactionary frame of mind.[14]

[6]

Such an antagonism of progressive vision and bureaucratic stasis or stylistic historicism was a familiar phenomenon in imperial Berlin. It was most tellingly depicted by preservationist photo initiatives of the last decades of the nineteenth century by the Royal Prussian Photogrammetric Institute (Königlich preussische Messbildanstalt) and professional photographers such as F. Albert Schwartz, who created a large number of photographs for the city museum of Berlin, the Märkische Museum. This small mid-nineteenth-century residence at the foot of the Kreuzberg [7], for example, must have caught Schwartz's keen eye for composition and the irony of urban change. It didn't survive Berlin's late-nineteenth-century urbanization, as it was in the way of a spectacular artificial waterfall, the highlight of the new Viktoriapark, which was built only a year after this photograph was taken. The tracing gesture and commemorative function of Schwartz's image is still present in the images of the Tränenpalast more than one hundred years later.

[7]

Both of today's images add to the interpretive layers of Berlin's more recent collective memory. One shows the palace hidden from the public eye as the experience of the disappearance of the oppressive East German regime slowly became part of the collective consciousness. The other one stands for a state of mind that was formed once that consciousness and the memory of East Germany had receded further but was also being more systematically addressed in academic, artistic, and public discourse. Memory and its recollection, the second image seems to suggest, is a fragile construct. Unless we practice a deliberate form of working through memory, that memory and part of one's identity is at risk of being distorted or rendered invisible. There is a German term for this process, *Erinnerungsarbeit*, which is used in the context of a critical acknowledgment of the Holocaust and of the role of fascism in Germany's postwar identity formation.

Similarly, the remnants of the Berlin Wall (plates 24 and 25 page 138/140), their disappearance, transplanting, sale to tourists as real or fake fragments, or monumentalization, speak about this city's mnemonic practices. These four images captured two stretches of the graffitied Wall, one looking northward toward the Television Tower, the other also looking north but from a spot further south along the Spree River. All four images capture the Wall at a dramatic diagonal, the former featuring it in the right image half (standing on its western side), the latter on the left (standing on its east side). Not much has changed about the Wall itself; but the images on the Wall have changed. In both cases, colorful graffiti have been replaced by what looks more like photographic renderings of urban landscapes and by text that appears to accompany the images for didactic purposes. In each diptych, the 2016 version features more people. They read and look at the Wall images or occupy the Spree's shore for leisure. The place along the Wall has morphed from a site that attracted a few tourists trying to hammer off a piece of the Wall as a souvenir into one of casual "edutainment"—a somewhat awkward merger of memorial site and tourist attraction.

It was the sociologist and philosopher Maurice Halbwachs who established that individual and collective memory are interdependent. In fact, they shift and are shaped by the amorphous input of impressions, recollections, and narratives. The memory of the Berlin Wall is nourished and molded by a different and wider range of people than the Palace of Tears. Yet other sites in Berlin might be even less recognizable as having any historical significance whatsoever. Lots of such places are captured in this book, but their presumed banality and insignificance appear in a different light from 2001 to 2016. "The Treehouse" at Bethaniendamm (plate 20 page 130) happens to be a monument of sorts, but one that emerged incidentally. The most striking change between these images is the growth of a couple of trees that this two-storied structure of detritus (plywood, metal scrap, window frames) was built around. A bit of research about this "garden" or "tree" house reveals that its original configuration was built by a Turkish guest worker named Osman Kalin in 1983 on land that, while accessible from West Berlin's Kreuzberg district, was actually no-man's-land. What was first a little Schrebergarten[15] for Kalin's large family turned into a geopolitical point of dispute after Berlin's reunification. It burned down twice, in 1991 and 2003, was first part of the Mitte District and slated for demolition, but saved through the initiative of friends and neighbors, and eventually redistricted to Kreuzberg. Today this spot is a tourist attraction. This volume's 2016 photograph of the site only hints at the 2003 burning, as the building's facade has noticeably changed. However, perhaps more remarkable is the street's brand-new cobblestone paving, clearly visible in 2016. Since the site was part of the border, that street surface originally was pieced together from different materials that were probably used to temporarily fix it while this place was in transition after 1989. Cobblestones were the original choice for street surfaces in Berlin, but they were often covered with asphalt after World War II to avoid noise and commotion from car traffic. Reintroducing cobblestones puts an official stamp of approval on this corner as a site of interest in the city, a tourist destination. It is governed by the same revivalism that led to the approval of the reconstruction of Berlin's historical city castle not far from The Treehouse.

Hyperculture Berlin during the past fifteen years has evolved into a city that accommodates what sociologist Andreas Reckwitz describes as an "expansive aestheticization [...] of lifestyles, an aestheticization of one's job and of one's personal relationships, of eating, living, traveling, and of the body, which are led by the ideals of a 'good life.'" In this environment, Reckwitz clarifies, culture is hyperculture, "in which potentially everything can become culturally valuable in a variety of ways."[16] Different temporalities converge in the Berlin photographs: the passage of time between 2001 and 2016, the speed of the instantaneous digital photograph, the time spent biking the city, through the observer's recollection and observation of these images from her own moment in time, time to follow the circular editorial choreography of the image sequence in the book, as well as through the city's position as part of a contemporary hyperculturalization. Different modes of time passage figure centrally in the city's culturalization. Reckwitz speaks of an opening culturalization, which shapes social (urban) structures. It is an important contributing factor to the formation and interpretation of the spaces of uncertainty as it is carried by subjective and emotional decisions and moves. Thinking of Berlin as its breeding ground offers a perspective on these Berlin photographs. It also reconnects us with Georg Simmel's related one-hundred-year-old observation of the city as a "site of 'qualitative individualism,' an individualism of uniqueness."[17] The speed of transformation, which these diptychs outline, is met with our expectations of what urban change is supposed to look like and how quickly it should take place. This almost instinctive impulse to compare and contrast plays out and is sometimes challenged in these images through a necessarily diligent comparative reading.

A neglected and lifeless urban site has been claimed by urban renewal in image plate 10 (page 110). An industrial no-man's-land alongside Berlin's S-Bahn tracks, with a couple of shabby barracks and a pragmatic gray sidewalk that served as a dumping ground for bright-blue garbage bags, is unrecognizable in the later photograph. Now the elevated train tracks are lined by a neatly paved pedestrian path. Restaurants and publicly accessible buildings open from under the track's vaulted spaces and from the other side of the path. This image's foreground is dominated by a group of young men with their bikes, who seem to be waiting for a friend who left his vehicle with them while taking care of an errand. This colorful (yellows, oranges, and pink spots garnish it) and sun-drenched image feels snapshot-like and promotional at the same time. It casually celebrates a leisurely middle-class lifestyle that has exploded all around in the gentrifying Mitte, Prenzlauer Berg and Friedrichshain districts.

Such dynamic and explicit demonstration of transformation is countered by image sets that coerce the viewer into slowdown. Comparing the first and second configuration of the city in such diptychs becomes an instructional exercise in deliberate viewing and visual literacy, as changes are subtle. The corner of Puttkamer and Friedrichstrasse in Kreuzberg (plate 21 page 132), for example, or the final image pair in the book, taken at Tempelhof Airfield

[8]

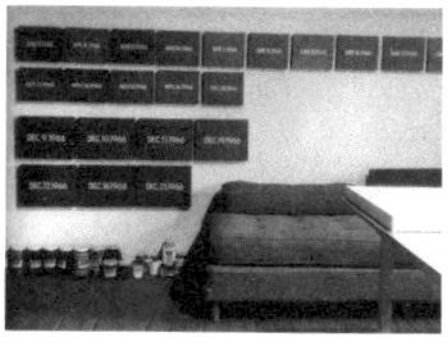

[9]

(plate 33 page 156), show sites that have changed very little. In each respective 2016 image, the site's motif is framed more tightly, the centrally featured street food stall on a bombed-out corner lot, and the billboard at the southwest entrance to the enormous runway of the former Tempelhof Airfield. Rather than thematizing the filling of urban voids or the potential for commemoration, these images read more like typologies in the vein of the German photographer couple Bernd and Hilla Becher [8] [18] or studies in the passage of time in the Date Paintings series [9] by the artist On Kawara. The Bechers established an organizing system by photographing industrial and rural structures such as water towers and blast furnaces and arranging them according to the building type in gallery spaces. The Japanese artist On Kawara painted small panels containing only the day's date on which they had been completed. He marked the moment and emphasized the process of painting as more important than the product of his activity.

Both temporality and the impulse to compare are embedded into the diptych. As a pair, the images trigger the art historian's impulse for an exhaustive comparison of two images that are shown or projected side by side in order to glean their iconographic meaning. This analytical strategy of comparative viewing was introduced to the discipline of art history by Heinrich Wölfflin (1864–1945), who was among the first to develop an art historical method of formal (stylistic) analysis. This volume's photographs invite such comparative analysis, not so much for their style but for the evidence of change they provide.

[10]

These photographs also share an even more obvious pictorial resemblance with the twin-image sets of the stereograph [10]. Popularized during the second half of the nineteenth century, they create the illusion of three-dimensionality by slightly shifting the photographer's viewpoint. However, the contemporary photographic stereoviews transport the viewer into an almost cinematic slow-motion experience. The stereogram of yesteryear was an enormously popular success because it convincingly created the spatial illusion of travel to faraway places, while today's diptychs deepen perception and internal reflection.

Aesthetics of Reappearance Virilio's pessimistic projection of an "overexposed city" in which "transparency has long supplanted appearances" and "the classical depth of field has been revitalized by the depth of time of advanced technologies," uttered in the 1980s, is now an established characterization of the moment when the screen and digital technology started to enter the public arena.[19] Today, a quarter century later, we have become accustomed to what felt like a technology-induced distortion. Being surrounded by the "depth of time and advanced technologies" has numbed our sense of the world, but it has also trained our coping mechanisms. While in Paris, the prototypical capital of modernity, "the parades on Haussmann Boulevard gave way to the Lumière brothers' accelerated motion picture inventions,"[20] Berlin's streets and squares today have become—yet again—exploration sites for the still photographic image, as the work of a number of contemporary artists demonstrates.[21] This volume's use of the medium and the diptych leads us back to what Virilio described as an "aesthetics of the appearance of a stable image" which is "present as an aspect of its static nature."[22] This regained stability's source is now most often the digital image with its unique relationship to space and time. However, the city and the photograph nevertheless experience a reversal of what Virilio calls the "transmutation of representations," which at once anchors and keeps us in a suspended pattern of uncertainty.[23]

Through various stages of a quasi-psychoanalytical working through of Berlin's topographical uncertainties and revelations of the different moments of its urban development, this book refocuses our attention on these sites, their history and transformation. They invite comparative viewing and exploration that takes their viewers far beyond their snapshot aesthetic, literally making these sites reappear. Our image-saturated subconscious's craving for deliberate retardation is being satisfied through a return to the diptych, and to a renewed commitment to observe. The photographs discussed here make these sites reappear because they work as means of critical discourse.

[Fig. 1] Georg Bartels, Rosenstraße, east side, November 2, 1894. Photograph, Landesarchiv Berlin, F Rep. 290-01-02 No. 74.

[Fig. 2] Georg Bartels, Rosenstraße, with a view of Marienkirche, 1896. Photograph. Inv. no. IV 68/479 V. © Stiftung Stadtmuseum Berlin, photograph by Michael Setzpfandt, Berlin.

[Fig. 3] Edouard Manet, ***Lunch on the Grass***, 1863. Oil on canvas, 208×264.5 cm. Inv. RF1668. Photo: Benoît Touchard / Mathieu Rabeau. Location: Musée d'Orsay, Paris, France. Photo Credit: © RMN-Grand Palais / Art Resource, NY Image Reference: ART481551.

[Fig. 4] Christian Boltanski, ***The Missing House*** (Grosse Hamburger Strasse, Berlin-Mitte), 1990.

[Fig. 5] Shimon Attie, ***The Writing on the Wall***, projections, 1992-93, Linienstrasse 137: Slide projection of police raid on former Jewish residents, 1920, Berlin, 1992, color photograph and on-location installation, © 2018 Artists Rights Society (ARS), New York / VG Bild-Kunst, Bonn; http://shimonattie.net/portfolio/the-writing-on-the-wall/#jp-carousel-1224.

[Fig. 6] Ludwig Mies van der Rohe, "Wabe," design for a skyscraper, Berlin Friedrichstrasse, 1922, Bauhaus-Archiv Berlin / © VG Bild-Kunst, Bonn 2016.

[Fig. 7] F. Albert Schwartz, view from Großbeerenstrasse southward toward the Kreuzberg, 1887. Photograph, Landesarchiv Berlin, Rep. 290-01-01-267.

[Fig. 8] Bernd and Hilla Becher, © Copyright, ***Water Towers***, 1980. Nine gelatin silver prints, approximately 61¼×49¼ in. (155.6×125.1 cm) overall. Purchased with funds contributed by Mr. and Mrs. Donald Jonas, 1981. Location: The Solomon R. Guggenheim Museum, New York, NY, USA. Photo Credit: The Solomon R. Guggenheim Foundation / Art Resource, NY Image Reference: ART457567.

[Fig. 9] On Kawara, Date Paintings. The artist's 13th Street Studio, New York, 1966, http://fnewsmagazine.com/2014/07/on-kawaras-last-days/; © Copyright David Zwirner Gallery.

[Fig. 10] Stereograph, Kroll's Garden Berlin, 1903.

1 John Armitage, "From Modernism to Hypermodernism and Beyond: An Interview with Paul Virilio," ***Theory, Culture & Society*** 16, nos. 5-6 (1999): 25-55; here, 43.

2 Andreas Huyssen, "The Voids of Berlin," ***Critical Inquiry*** 24, no. 1 (Autumn 1997): 57-81.

3 Armitage, "From Modernism to Hypermodernism," 41 (see note 1).

4 Ibid., 26.

5 Siegfried Kracauer, "Über Arbeitsnachweise," ***Frankfurter Zeitung***, June 17, 1930: "Jeder typische Raum wird durch die typischen gesellschaftlichen Verhältnisse zustande gebracht, die sich ohne die störende Dazwischenkunft des Bewußtseins in ihm ausdrücken. Alles vom Bewußtsein Verleugnete, alles, was sonst geflissentlich übersehen wird, ist an seinem Aufbau beteiligt. Die Raumbilder sind die Träume der Gesellschaft. Wo immer die Hieroglyphe irgendeines Raumbildes entziffert ist dort bietet sich der Grund der sozialen Wirklichkeit dar." [my translations unless otherwise noted]

6 Indeed, other parts of this project align and can be interpreted as part of a magnificent body of urban photographic work that grew exponentially during the last two decades of the nineteenth and the first decade of the twentieth centuries. Interesting cases in point are the works of photographers such as Bartels, but also of F. Albert Schwartz, Hugo Rudolphy, Heinrich Zille, Max Missmann, and Waldemar Titzenthaler, who each with their own particular style and formal preferences documented the imperial city in rapid transformation.

7 Max Osborn, "Ein Berliner Bilderarchiv von Max Osborn," ***Der Tag***, July 13, 1910, n.p. My translation. "Man erkennt, daß vor unseren Augen aus dem allzu schnell gewachsenen Gemeinwesen, dem das Parvenutum und die Großmannssucht aus allen Poren schwitzten, eine wirkliche Weltstadt, aus dem Wirrwarr ein modernes Leben von Charakter, aus der Ratlosigkeit nach und nach ein Organismus entsteht."

8 See, for example, Andreas Huyssen, ***Present Pasts: Urban Palimpsests and the Politics of Memory*** (Stanford: Stanford University Press, 2003).

9 See James E. Young, "Daniel Libeskind's Jewish Museum in Berlin: The Uncanny Arts of Memorial Architecture," ***Jewish Social Studies***, n.s., 6, no. 2 (Winter 2000): 1-23; James E. Young, "Memory and Counter-Memory: The End of the Monument in Germany," ***Harvard Design Magazine***, no. 9 (Fall 1999): 1-10; and Anthony Vidler, "Building in Empty Spaces: Daniel Libeskind and the Postspatial Void," in ***Warped Space: Art, Architecture, and Anxiety in Modern Culture*** (Cambridge, MA: MIT Press, 2000), 235-42.

10 See Abigail Solomon-Godeau, "Mourning or Melancholia: Christian Boltanski's ***Missing House***," ***Oxford Art Journal*** 21, no. 2 (1998): 3-20.

11 See Shimon Attie, "The Writing on the Wall, Berlin, 1992-93: Projections in Berlin's Jewish Quarter," ***Art Journal*** 62, no. 3 (Autumn 2003): 74-83.

12 See Jennifer A. Jordan, ***Structures of Memory: Understanding Urban Change in Berlin and Beyond*** (Stanford: Stanford University Press, 2006).

13 This design was dubbed "Wabe" (honeycomb) for its cellular interior. See Gideon Haigh, ***The Office: A Hardworking History*** (Victoria: The Miegunyah Press, 2012), 169.

14 Johanna Adorján, "Das Haus, das keiner wollte," ***Frankfurter Allgemeine Zeitung***, January 10, 2011, http://www.faz.net/aktuell/feuilleton/architektur-in-berlin-mitte-das-haus-das-keiner-wollte-1577944.html.

15 The Schrebergarten (Schreber Garden) was named after the German Daniel Gottlieb Moritz Schreber (1808-1861), an early promoter of naturopathy. After Schreber's death, the teacher Heinrich Karl Gesell developed small garden lots,

originally set up to teach gardening to children, which were soon taken over by their parents, who planted fruits and vegetables.

16 Andreas Reckwitz, "Zwischen Hyperkultur und Kulturessenzialismus," ***Soziopolis***, October 24, 2016, accessed May 2, 2017, https://soziopolis.de/daten/kalenderblaetter/beobachten/kultur/artikel/zwischen-hyperkultur-und-kulturessenzialismus/.

17 Ibid., Quoted after Georg Simmel: Soziologie Untersuchungen über die Formen der Vergesellschaftung (Berlin: Duncker & Humblot, 1908). Accessed July 29, 2017, http://socio.ch/sim/soziologie/soz_10.htm.

18 See an overview of their work in Blake Stimson, "The Photographic Comportment of Bernd and Hilla Becher," ***Tate Papers***, no. 1 (Spring 2004), accessed May 9, 2017, http://www.tate.org.uk/research/publications/tate-papers/01/photographic-comportment-of-bernd-and-hilla-becher.

19 Paul Virilio, ***The Lost Dimension***, trans. Daniel Moshenberg (New York City: Semiotext(e), 1991), 25.

20 Ibid.

21 See, for example, work by Wiebke Loeper, Maria Sewcz, Elisabeth Neudörfl, Michael Schmidt, Thomas Florschuetz, and Florian Profitlich.

22 Virilio, ***The Lost Dimension***, 25 (see note 19). This precinematic state was, according to Virilio, surpassed by the "aesthetics of the disappearance of an unstable image—present in its cinematic and cinematographic flight of escape."

23 Ibid.

"As they multiply, these signs of rebirth, urbanity, and ingenuity raise more and more the question: Are we witnessing a golden age of urban reclamation? Or, as the concept of reclamation already suggests, a singular and especially cynical revanchism?"

From the Terrain Vague to the Tyranny of Place *Mariana Mogilevich*

Twenty-first century urbanism, so far, appears to be a practice of filling in the blanks. In the more affluent cities of the developed world, it seems that every parking lot, every vacant lot, parking space, traffic intersection, abandoned industrial facility, and waterfront has been transformed into a new place. Temporary installations of café tables and chairs, vegetable gardens, and food trucks quickly become contemporary art centers, parks, and new apartments. As they multiply, these signs of rebirth, urbanity, and ingenuity raise more and more the question: Are we witnessing a golden age of urban reclamation? Or, as the concept of reclamation already suggests, a singular and especially cynical revanchism?

The twenty-first century began with modernity—and urbanism—superannuated and evacuated. As suburbanization and deindustrialization reached a climax, the Western metropolis was increasingly defined by what it lacked. The twin poles of the *terrain vague* and the non-place marked an end to the city as the dense meeting place of strangers and the collective work of citizens. On the one hand were the empty and unproductive voids of an anxious metropolitan landscape; on the other, the repetitive, global landscape of shopping mall and airport, totally devoid of meaning and social life.[1] The denizens of these landscapes of exclusion were the homeless and the alienated.

Yet hardly two decades later we find ourselves under the opposite sign. In the wealthy cities that seemed to have outlived their usefulness, with every intersection a plaza and elevated highway turned park, the margins that were ripe for inclusion and experimentation have become entrenched in formula. Projects that began with citizens (or those who felt disenfranchised as citizens) making space for themselves—rehabilitating and appropriating abandoned, leftover, or traffic-centered spaces for their own needs and desires—have become a matter of generalized policy and urban practice. The humble techniques of the amateur—or as they've been coined, *tactics*—have been enthusiastically taken up by professionals of various stripes. As the urbanists would have it, everywhere is a community ready to be empowered. Planners have engendered how-to guides for "tactical urbanism," which they describe as "an approach to neighborhood activation using short-term, low-cost, and scalable interventions and policies."[2] Placemaking professionals expand their practice worldwide, leading workshops for those who would learn how to "turn a place around," and consulting for city governments and international organizations. As their influence spreads, critics have begun to characterize these practitioners as "placetakers" who are in fact propelling and covering up the disenfranchisement of urban dwellers through their creative and feel-good interventions.[3] It is the tyranny of place.

This trajectory from the *terrain vague* to the tyranny of place is encapsulated in before-and-after photographs. The representational device is not an original strategy; in the past it was used to document and display decrepit slums replaced by sleek boulevards or towers. The difference in contemporary scenes is that nothing is replaced, only embellished with certain common tropes of urbanity, defined as social interaction or, at a minimum, copresence in urban space. The before-and-after aerial photographs of the transformation of New York City's Times Square from vehicular crossroads to a pedestrian plaza are a good example. In photographs that have become ubiquitous, the side-by-side comparison of a road filled with snarling traffic and a plaza of sprawled-out tourists flattens a political and spatial process into a blink of an eye, in the style of the home renovation makeovers popular in the heyday of reality television. Since 2008 New York City's Department of Transportation has, by means of planters, gravel, tables, and chairs, converted seventy-three underused roadway sections into pedestrian plazas. The city pays for design, materials, and construction; local sponsors must then operate, maintain, and manage the space, securing insurance, paying for cleaning, and organizing programming.

The image of the Times Square intervention shares a certain can-do spirit with those of citizens painting their own crosswalks or converting parking spaces into miniature parks. It reads as community-driven, especially if, like the advocates of tactical urbanism, one dissociates tactics from their potential as weapons of the weak to argue that tactics are not for those who have no other recourse, but for everyone, including, explicitly, governments and real estate developers who benefit from doing things that appear bottom-up, backstory be damned.[4] Rather than community action, the new Times Square (and the citywide program of plazas to which it corresponds) is the fruit of a commissioned report by Gehl, formerly Gehl Architects, and presently an international consultancy on making "cities for people." In such cities, the role people play is not behind the scenes, but cheerily sitting in their chairs, as captured in the photographs. When people engage in other forms of urban activity, such as tactics to secure a livelihood, planners and politicians panic. The appearance of scantily-clad and salty-tongued street performers in 2015, a return of Times Square's repressed, almost led the city to restore the area to vehicular traffic. Indeed, these street performers were subsequently limited to "designated activity zones" established by the plaza's private management partner. These were a second-order tactical intervention, eight 10 × 50-foot boxes within the pedestrian plaza, marked off on the asphalt with the application of green paint.

The Evolution of Marginal Practice In 1963 urban designer Kevin Lynch wrote an essay celebrating the opportunities at the urban margins, "The Openness of Open Space." He pointed designers to look beyond urban parks and formal open spaces to vacant lots and disused waterfronts as grounds for freedom of action and individual development. In a modern metropolis that was beyond the grasp and the control of the citizen, these leftover spaces provided room for the insertion of human desire and agency. Lynch anticipated some of the promise of an emancipatory and participatory urbanism that would flourish later in that decade, when temporary occupations and visions of a beach beneath the streets animated youth around the globe. In declining cities in the United States, gardens in vacant lots and disused waterfront piers made room for community and the expression of identity for new migrants to the city, whether Spanish speakers from colonized Puerto Rico or gay men and women from conservative small towns. Where it was abandoned, ignored, or left over, those with few recourses could claim and shape space to their own desires.

Armchair sociologist and planning guru William H. Whyte also saw opportunity in the vacant lots and city streets of the 1960s and 1970s: they were ripe for reuse as public space. Whyte envisioned a city of heightened sociability, where people felt comfortable to linger and interact. He promoted new corporate atria and privately managed parks for them to do so in New York and other cities in the decades that followed. These spaces were safe, exclusive, and attractive to corporations and commuters. White-collar workers were migrants, too—or at least mobile. Their movement into or out of the central business district could make or break an urban economy weakened by suburbanization, incipient globalization, and reduced public spending. Rather than opening up the city to all comers, the social life for which Whyte argued in small urban spaces opened the city up for redevelopment. The activation of certain margins and interstices promoted interaction and a sense of urbane exchange, at the cost of greater exclusion. This sociability was managed by private entities and maintainers of public order who controlled for undesirables, a category which started with drug users and sellers and the homeless but easily expanded to include everyone except paying customers as privatization extended its reach.

It was in response to this revanchist urbanism that, in the 1990s, some urban theorists and designers turned their attention and praise to a new urbanism of the everyday. This was the urbanism of vendors and squatters, practitioners of bricolage, autoconstruction, and *arts de faire*.[5] It was more often than not the making-do of migrants, from Filipina domestic workers gathering in the space under a Hong Kong skyscraper to Central Americans farming guavas and papayas in the vacant lots of Los Angeles. Opportunistically filling the voids left over by urban development, they offered the promise of alternative, even guerrilla public spaces. Because their city-making was spontaneous and participatory, theorists saw such spaces as more open and inclusive than conventional, single-user, consumption-oriented public spaces.

The presence of immigrants in large numbers has been remaking cities global and provincial. It is concurrent with another migratory explosion of the turn of the millennium, the embrace of the city by a group christened the creative class. According to Richard Florida, middle-class professionals are the backbone of a movement back to the city from suburban environments, in search of urbanity and diversity.[6] In many cases, creatives—in reality the same white-collar professionals who haunted Whyte's city—have been drawn to the same places as the migrants escaping economic precarity and political and social oppression. They, too, creatively appropriate leftover spaces for more gathering space or a more responsive urban policy. Urban beaches and parking lot food festivals figure among the adaptive reuse and reclamation that attract creatives as residents and tourists.

As these practices have expanded, they have resulted in what architecture critic Rowan Moore has called "monocle urbanism," in reference to the global lifestyle publication which tracks the urban "quality of life" for a hypermobile public. The image of a maker/leisure/shopping space composed of reused shipping containers on a formerly industrial site is familiar from Atlanta to Lisbon.[7] This increasingly tedious assemblage looks like—but is not—a grassroots construction of urban sociability. If the protagonists of the millennial city started by creatively filling in blanks where there was opportunity for transformation, today they are more likely to be coloring inside the lines of a pattern book deployed from city to city by real estate interests seeking to attract a particular genre of economic actor.

The most familiar illustration of the conflicting and contradictory effects of a globalized urbanism of the margins can be found at the High Line, a project whose development perfectly tracks early twenty-first-century urbanism. In 1999 a group of New York City residents organized to promote the preservation and adaptive reuse of a fragment of industrial infrastructure at the western edge of Manhattan. What began as a citizen-led microproject opened to the public ten years later after an international design competition, millions of dollars in donations, and a new public-private partnership to build and manage the site. The High Line jump-started a speculation and construction boom that transformed the surrounding area into a playground for rich residents and visitors. At the same time, it contributed to the alienation of lower-income neighbors, who, according to a city report, "felt profound anxiety" and "a loss" at the changes in the neighborhood.[8] The famous "before" photographs of the High Line's elevated tracks as an unplanned terrain of urban nature compare favorably with the "after", where new construction and tourists seem to close in on the linear park. In its brief history, the High Line has spawned a thousand imitations across the globe, from São Paulo to Chicago. It has also inspired soul searching about how to adapt industrial landscapes for public use without catalyzing the displacement we call gentrification. At the original site, the private friends group that developed and now manages the park is "now thinking about what it would mean to view all its work from a social justice and equity perspective," according to a consultant to the Friends of the High Line.[9] It is an acknowledgment that the recovery of the margins, as a practice by which those with little power could not only occupy but determine social space, is almost inherently at odds with that possibility today.

Place or Process Like the reuse of marginal urban open space, gentrification is a phenomenon with strong roots in the 1960s and 1970s that has become a principal aspect of twenty-first-century urbanism, even as its imagination far outpaces the reality. So powerful is the fear of gentrification that in neighborhoods in a few United States cities, almost any physical improvement in public space is met with hostility and anxiety. An envisioning process for a space under a highway overpass or a street map celebrating community assets could be the first hint of a new wave of displacement via placemaking. The creation of place is tyrannical in that it dictates an approach to neighborhood improvement that is not so much an opportunity for residents to engage their city as producers, as it is a ploy to be engaged in a process in which they have no agency—thus the growing perception that even the cheapest and quickest of upgrades to a neighborhood's public space is intended not for an existing public, but a future one envisioned by the state and real estate actors. All projects are portents of gentrification.

So, if the "end of big" (as tactical urbanists echo the 1970s cry of "small is beautiful" without the call for an economic system that puts human needs first) is not necessarily cause for celebration, is a micropolitics of place to be defended, or avoided? In urbanism as in politics, there are different sides to populism, many of them dark. The suspicion of bottom-up urbanism is not unfounded. It begs the question: For whose creativity is there room in the city today? In many instances, marginalized residents are enlisted to provide time, labor, and energy to transform marginal spaces over which they nonetheless forfeit control. But the conclusion that no benefits, upgrades, or change at all is preferable to a future of place-based transformation is a bleak perspective. Better my vacant lot than someone else's park, seems to be the position.

If the small-scale and the place-based appear as a Trojan horse for long-term demographic transformation and ultimately diminished claims to space by urban residents, there are still alternatives in small-scale initiatives that conceive their influence across a network and that focus not on physical interventions but on the processes and policies that inform and maintain them. This is another kind of strategy. When New York inaugurated its program of municipal plazas in traffic intersections across the city, it left individual neighborhoods to make and manage them, putting business improvement associations in the driver's seat and promising to propagate a new inequality in the city's public space. The nonprofit Neighborhood Plaza Partnership has since stepped in to advocate lasting civic commons beyond the neighborhoods where they served business owners looking for increased foot traffic, to provide maintenance and technical assistance, and to make the case for regular financial support from the city. As important as the spaces or their publics are the institutions that manage the relationships between them.

In Corona, Queens, a neighborhood where 64 percent of residents are foreign-born and have limited financial resources and limited influence on local government, the Queens Museum spearheaded a program of community engagement around the development of a new pedestrian plaza in the space next to an elevated subway track where moving trucks idled between jobs. The museum did not hatch plans for Corona Plaza as a pleasant physical improvement; the project developed out of a series of discussions with neighborhood residents and organizations about their needs. The museum then planned and designed the plaza to serve those multiple needs: for health services, space for community organizations and locally relevant and produced programming, and more public space for both families and single men unwelcome elsewhere. Ultimately, the plaza is an experiment in creating a dignified public space for immigrants, motivated by the creativity of residents and migrants, and conceived and developed not to engage them as spectators but as its producers (and attentive to the division of labor in creating and maintaining the space).[10] Framing the role of professionals—artists, architects, planners, and community organizers—as engaged not in placemaking but place finding, and strengthening and making visible what is already present in a neighborhood, the museum has expanded its work to advocate immigrants' rights to other public spaces. And it has presented its process for Corona Plaza as a model for other organizations to follow, so that the plaza is not one instance of an opportunistic reappropriation, but an alternative vision for the role that cultural institutions can play in their communities.

Even in Corona, the start of construction for a permanent plaza has raised fears and warnings of what a new place might bring. But if the reclamation of urban margins has proven an effective strategy for urban redevelopment, conceived otherwise, and under a different model of production, it still harbors the potential to make urban space in the image of its residents. Groups and institutions play a critical role, not as catalysts for physical transformation, but to the extent that they can safeguard the processes and rules that guide such spaces' function and governance. Activist groups in many cities are identifying and fighting for access to fallow land, not only to put it to community use, but to preserve it under collective or state ownership. In this way they can regulate future development and lay the groundwork for the creation and protection of an urban commons. The marginal spaces they mine not only hold the potential to be transformed for collective use; they can be the basis for building power to transform something bigger—the structures and processes that marginalize some spaces and some people to begin with.

1 See Marc Augé, ***Non-Places: An Introduction to Supermodernity*** (New York: Verso, 1995); Ignasi de Solà-Morales, "Terrain Vague," in ***Anyplace***, ed. Cynthia Davidson (Cambridge, MA: MIT Press, 1995); Antoine Picon, "Anxious Landscapes: From the Ruin to Rust," ***Grey Room***, no. 1 (September 2000): 64-83.

2 Mike Lydon and Anthony Garcia, ***Tactical Urbanism: Short-Term Action for Long-Term Change*** (Washington, DC: Island Press, 2015), 24.

3 See Sean M. Starowitz and Julia Cole, "Thoughts on Creative Placetaking," ***Lumpen*** 125 (Summer 2015): 34-41.

4 Lydon and Garcia, ***Tactical Urbanism***, 27-28 (see note 2).

5 See, for example, John Chase, Margaret Crawford, and John Kaliski, eds., ***Everyday Urbanism*** (New York: Monacelli Press, 1999); James Holston, ed., ***Cities and Citizenship*** (Durham: Duke University Press, 1998); Jeffrey Hou, ed., ***Insurgent Public Space: Guerrilla Urbanism and the Remaking of Contemporary Cities*** (New York: Routledge, 2010).

6 See Richard Florida, ***The Rise of the Creative Class*** (New York: Basic Books, 2002).

7 See Rowan Moore, "How Down-at-heel Lisbon Became the New Capital of Cool," ***Guardian***, April 16, 2017.

8 Mireya Navarro, "In Chelsea, a Great Wealth Divide," ***New York Times***, October 23, 2015.

9 Danya Sherman, "Creating a More Equitable High Line," ***High Line Magazine*** (March 1, 2017), accessed June 10, 2017, http://www.thehighline.org/blog/2017/03/01/high-line-magazine-creating-a-more-equitable-high-line.

10 See Valeria Mogilevich, Mariana Mogilevich, and Queens Museum staff, ***Corona Plaza Es Para Todos: Making a Dignified Public Space for Immigrants*** (New York: Queens Museum, 2016).

"While temporary use is still seen as a way to transgress formalized participation by offering direct engagement and on-site experimentation, it has also been framed as complicit with neoliberalization and its rhetoric of responsibilization."

Rethinking Temporary Use in the Neoliberal City *Philipp Misselwitz*

Top-Down and Bottom-Up Since its emergence in the late nineteenth century, modern city planning has been shaped by a dualistic perspective, which has been variably described by the oppositions of regulation and laissez-faire, top-down and bottom-up, formal planning and informal development. To some extent, life in cities and urban areas has always been a negotiation between control and the reality of its limits. But in its resolute idealism, modern planners approached the formal as strictly positive and discredited the informal as something to be absolutely avoided. This way of seeing was fueled by the rapid and unbridled growth of industrial centers that produced densely inhabited and polluted slums. The excesses of laissez-faire capitalism, it was thought, could only be countered by a tabula rasa. The planning equivalent of the call for regulation and government intervention was the city designed on the drawing board. From then on, the traditional role of the informal as usefully coexisting with the formal was abandoned, and the top-down approach became the new orthodoxy.

This orthodoxy continues to shape our understanding of history. In Berlin and other cities throughout Europe, informal barrack settlements on the outskirts of the city and the informal housing of workers and migrants persisted, despite the ambitions of modern planners. In the wake of the world economic crisis at the end of the 1920s, wild settlements and practices of self-construction were real options for urban life. Nevertheless, they were scarcely documented and largely ignored as an unintended shadow of modernity, soon to be eradicated. Yet urban societies in the bombed city centers of post–World War I Europe could only survive due to the self-provisioning of emergency housing and nonregulated food production. Allotment gardens became essential oases for survival. Even though some architects recognized the important role of self-provisioning and self-building in future development, the mainstream narrative of modernism remains one of heroic comprehensive planning. Self-provisioning did not become part of the mainstream discourse on how to rebuild destroyed cities after World War I, and neither did it after World War II.

It was only with the crisis of Fordism and Keynesianism in the Western liberal democracies in the 1960s that the orthodox approach of modern planning was criticized as paternalistic and authoritarian. In Berlin, the newly built Institute of Architecture at the Technical University became a spiritual center and stage of critique and revolt, calling for a radical rethinking of architectural education and practice as a political as well as inter- and transdisciplinary endeavor. Many of the active students were also squatters in Kreuzberg and used the ruins abandoned by modern planning as practical testing spaces for alternative, system-critical utopias. Inspired by critics such as Jane Jacobs in her groundbreaking 1961 book *The Death and Life of Great American Cities*, students were able to approach everyday urban life as a laboratory, offering invaluable learning for planners and architects.[1] In his book *The Possible City* (1968), Kevin Lynch conjured up the possibilities of the existing, unfinished, and failed city: "We can explore the use of streets as play areas, or the possibilities for using roof tops, empty stores, abandoned buildings, waste lots, odd bits of land, or the large areas presently sterilized by such monocultures as parking lots, expressways, railroad yards, and airports."[2] In the decades that followed, the ideas of Jacobs and Lynch found application in mainstream planning codes and urban policies, albeit in much less radical form.

Planning orthodoxy in West Berlin—and West Germany—changed accordingly, away from top-down tabula rasa planning to embrace the paradigm of the heterogeneous, organically evolving city. The International Building Exhibition of 1984–87 in Berlin was key in this shift, repositioning debates not only about the planning process but also about architectural form. Yet the building boom following the reunification of Berlin in the subsequent decade shows how quickly the paradigm of an organically evolving city can transform into a dull formal-aesthetic set of standards and codes. The idea of urban heterogeneity, initially postulated by activists as a mode of resistance against modern planning, was co-opted by planners and frozen in a rigid design charter. The Berlin model of the Critical Reconstruction and the Planwerk Innenstadt (Plan for the inner city) concept amount to a return to top-down control disguised as an attempt to save the European city. On closer inspection, however, this experiment turns out to have had limited success. By the end of the 1990s, the gap between planning ideals and urban reality could not have been greater. Directly after the fall of the Berlin Wall, city planners had assumed strong population growth, and numerous master plans for inner-city developments were commissioned. Yet only a few of these plans were actually implemented. After a short construction boom in the first half of the 1990s, planning deadlocks and urban vacancies persisted throughout the city. Many plans just remained plans, albeit at great public expense and accumulating public debt, while the much more significant urban transformations and reinventions, which had such a profound impact on my own generation, took place in vacant spaces where planning seemed to fail.

Triumph of the Temporary? In cities like Berlin or Leipzig, urban wastelands that could not be absorbed by traditional redevelopment project approaches existed in abundance. What seemed like a defect from the established planning perspective became an opportunity for a new set of mainly young urban actors. Spaces were claimed, appropriated, and used with the simplest means. Whatever already existed was pragmatically appropriated and reinterpreted. Unlike in the 1970s, the aim was not so much to create politicized counterworlds; instead, open and often dynamically growing clusters with colorful mixtures of programs emerged. Profit-making was rarely the main aim, as long as some returns paid for essential expenses.

It did not last too long before the successes of these temporary use practices appeared on the radar screen of city officials. First to take note were economists and regeneration teams; then came the planners. The process of gradual integration and institutionalization of temporary use practices into mainstream planning discourse was recently traced by the research project InnoPlan.[3] After initial hesitation and cautious toleration, many city administrations, authorities, and even ministries have now opened up to the phenomenon. Temporary use actors spectacularly metamorphosed, in the eyes of planners, from enfants terribles to "Raumpioniere," who can generate value for the city.[4] Temporary uses suddenly became synonymous with the creative potential of a city and a competitive advantage. The fear of a brain drain of creative minds to other cities triggered city-led initiatives to provide additional spaces for alternative development paths including Munich (Dachauer Strasse), Hamburg (Oberhafencity) or Basel (Klybeckquai), to name a few. Even the national building code was modified to follow suit (see the amendment of the BauGB in 2004 with the addition of § 9, para. 2, "Temporary Construction"). Many cities like Wuppertal and Bremen set up temporary use agencies linked to municipal governance structures but with some considerable freedom to strike deals with user groups of designated sites. In general, German municipal planning became more dialogic. Charrettes, round tables, and cooperative planning processes seem to be increasingly favored models to address local planning challenges as the bureaucratized and overregulated participation formats of established planning processes are no longer considered sufficient. Within this trend, temporary use continues to play a key part, offering formats of direct inclusion within and beyond expert-driven planning processes. The number of positive, partly euphoric appraisals of temporary use, largely promoted by municipal administrations or nonprofit foundations, seem to be evidence of the transition of the ephemeral into the planning mainstream.[5]

In light of this apparent success story one might be tempted to declare a profound paradigm shift in planning. But is the mainstreaming of temporary use really indicative of a fundamental change in values toward planning that might, once and for all, reconcile the dualism between bottom-up and top-down? Have we entered a new era where bottom-up practices are no longer opposing top-down planning, where the unregulated, everyday life practices of citizens with their potential to trigger incremental and organic change processes have been institutionalized within actor-oriented, people-centered approaches? In 2015 Berlin celebrated the voting down of the Tempelhof referendum with a festival called "Make City." Yet within the euphoria, critical voices emerged which have long since overtaken the optimists.[6] It is time to consider their arguments.

Opportunities and Risks in the Neoliberal City It is broadly acknowledged that temporary use has allowed new actors to engage in urban development processes. The spectrum of urban practices has become more colorful and diverse. But many critics point to misunderstandings and frequent idealizations with regard to who these actors are and what motivates them. For most cities or real estate owners, the potential to yield long-term economic benefits through temporary use practices remains crucial. The creative economy argument resonated well in an increasingly entrepreneurial city.[7] Private property owners quickly learned how to exploit the image of the improvised and ephemeral provided by temporary use practices as a competitive advantage to rebrand sites and attract potential tenants and buyers. Many critics point to the way the creative economy perspective on temporary use leads to a distortion of spatial practices that once transgressed profit and nonprofit approaches: mostly those temporary uses are privileged which can easily be accommodated within profit-oriented development. Others are left to themselves and often quickly displaced. This argument resonates within a broader neoliberalization critique within liberal Western democracies, which points to a changing role of the state no longer as the sole (re)distributor of public welfare and resources. Instead, more and more decision-making in urban change processes is left to nonstate actors. From the perspective of this critique, localization, projectization, and decentralization of planning is no longer a breakthrough of the bottom-up, but a worrying restructuring that leaves powerful nonstate actors in charge without the necessary guardrails, leading to the takeover of the market with financialization and commodification creeping into all aspects of urban management and city life. So is this the ultimate co-optation of the bottom-up and of temporary use as a planning strategy? In what follows, I suggest two different questions to move forward.

1. To what extent do "spatial entrepreneurs" serve the public good?

I argue that we need a less idealistic, self-aggrandizing understanding of who is likely to become a spatial entrepreneur engaged in temporary use practices. Many critics point to structural determinants, which are often overlooked when focusing on the agency and creativity of individuals. The urban sociologist Erik Swyngedouw, for instance, suspects that most actors belong to a rather narrow, already privileged societal elite—the "High Bohème" of our society, with the time, budgets, educational backgrounds, and resources to engage and take leadership in local projects.[8] Others would argue that spatial entrepreneurs are themselves victims of structural changes in the economy and employment cultures—part of a self-exploiting precariat.[9] The abandonment of traditional work structures is indeed reflected in the biographies of today's temporary users. They often switch between project-related work, unpaid commitment, unemployment, undeclared work, temporary employment, and part-time employment. While many municipalities reduce local neighborhood presence, some temporary users fill in the gap. While redirected public funding for local cultural or educational programs might help to sustain local nonprofit initiatives and can lead to more imaginative activities, the protagonists themselves are rarely paid sufficiently and remain in permanent limbo with regard to their own job security.

In any case, temporary use initiatives change power constellations at the local level and therefore naturally trigger conflicts over the way they might occupy public land and attract and/or divert state resources such as funding. What might be intended as community-oriented can be perceived by others as purely motivated by self-interest. Commoning practices deliberately or unconsciously generate new forms of exclusion and might fuel conflicts between local constituencies. Hence, temporary use initiatives have been associated by many with early signs of local gentrification processes. Kreuzberg and Neukölln have shown that artists' studios, coworking spaces, the club scene, bars, and cafés greatly enrich the life of a neighborhood but also trigger real estate speculation and displacement processes. In the eyes of the New York-based sociologist Sharon Zukin, the belief in the self-regulating power of local neighborhoods so eloquently articulated by Jane Jacobs decades before appears flawed. Revisiting central Manhattan, neighborhoods once saved by Jacobs from modernist tabula rasa destruction have been gentrified, with local diversity reduced to a mere aesthetic veneer.[10] We now know from transformation pathways of cities like Berlin and New York that a pure laissez-faire based on a naïve belief in the virtues of bottom-up can lead to dead ends; alternative spatial practices do not necessarily lead to democratization but can also destroy diversity and heterogeneity. We will not be able to bypass the permanent question, What is the right balance of top-down and bottom-up?

2. How "cooperative" are the new local planning processes? While planning processes have undoubtedly become more process-oriented, did the mainstreaming of temporary use planning lead to an actual power shift toward the grassroots level? Have the many new cooperative and communicative planning tools—the charrette rounds, the round tables, and the stakeholder processes that have almost become a new orthodoxy in planning—really altered the distribution of power? Once again, a more critical, conflict-sensitive perspective might be helpful to break through widespread idealization. New coproduction processes, one might argue, make the mindsets of planners, architects, and experts collide even more directly with the logic of the market and the interests of civil society groups of individual local inhabitants. Do new formats then lead to a new sharing of power? Has subversion or co-optation become more difficult? A brief discussion of recent planning conflicts around the former Berlin-Tempelhof Airfield shows that an easy answer might be difficult. After the closure of the airfield in 2008, city planning officials were initially prepared to launch an experiment. For the first time in Berlin, nonprofit-oriented temporary use became a consciously applied instrument in a redevelopment strategy for the large public park. "Pioneering fields" were opened to local initiatives and individuals in 2010. The runway became a site for temporary installations. The approach received local and international acclaim. However, the perceived harmony between the Senate and local temporary use initiatives was short-lived. Already in 2011, the Senate started to prepare plans for a large-scale housing development around the periphery of the airfield, meeting large-scale local opposition and triggering an unprecedented plebiscite that eventually shelved the development plans, which would have included a major new city library, residential and commercial property (including low-income housing), and plans for an international gardening exhibition. But it would be wrong and hasty to assume here a victory of temporary use over conventional top-down planning.

Recent planning conflicts such as Tempelhof, Stuttgart 21, or the bid for the 2024 Olympics in Hamburg in 2015 (which was also canceled after a local plebiscite) seem to point to a shift toward citizen power and more dialogic planning. Nevertheless, most cities detect here less a new model and paradigm than a crisis and threat. As a consequence, cities invest in new communication tools and building public support. How, ask experts, are key strategic challenges such as housing or refugee crises, climate-change adaptation, or dispute resolution solved, if necessary and sometimes even difficult decisions fail on the NIMBY (Not In My Back Yard) behavior of the local population? Did the negotiation processes mean a further weakening of the state? Does too much bottom-up lead to deficits in democracy and solidarity and thus act as a threat to the common good and the interests of those who are weaker? Erik Swyngedouw suggests an answer to these questions in his analysis of stakeholder governance in the context of neoliberalization processes in European cities.[11] Here he uses the notion of Janus: Localism leads to both positive and problematic effects. In fact, there is still a great lack of understanding about the actual perspectives and rationalities of temporary users and their medium- and long-term effects in urban neighborhoods. These are important questions that can be interesting for universities, which can accompany critical planning processes and urban transformation processes: How much determination and control, how much openness and indeterminacy are necessary?

Our gaze at Berlin's open spaces seems therefore less celebratory, even somewhat burdened and polarizing today. To some, they still offer ways to transgress formalized and contested consultation and participation models by offering the potential for direct engagement and on-site experimentation. To others, the critique of temporary use as related to processes of neoliberalization draws attention to issues of responsibilization. In an attempt to transgress these binaries, I would argue for a more nuanced, case-by-case assessment of the potential of temporary appropriation of vacant space in order to make our cities more diverse, engaging, and just. The right balance of bottom-up and top-down has to be renegotiated not only by every society and every generation, but also in relation to local contexts.

Philipp Oswalt, Klaus Overmeyer, and Philipp Misselwitz, ***Urban Catalyst: The Power of Temporary Use*** (Berlin: DOM, 2013).

1 Jane Jacobs, ***The Death and Life of Great American Cities*** (New York: Random House, 1961).

2 Kevin Lynch, "The Possible City," in ***City Sense and City Design: Writings and Projects of Kevin Lynch***, ed. T. Banerjee and M. Southworth (Cambridge, MA: MIT Press, 1995), 771-88; here, 776.

3 See Thomas Honeck, "Zwischennutzung als soziale Innovation: Von alternativen Lebensentwürfen zu Verfahren der räumlichen Planung," ***Informationen zur Raumentwicklung*** 3 (2015): 219-31.

4 See Klaus Overmeyer, ***Urban Pioneers*** (Berlin: Jovis Verlag, 2007).

5 See ibid.; Kristien Ring, AA PROJECTS, and Senatsverwaltung für Stadtentwicklung und Umwelt, Berlin, eds., ***Selfmade City*** (Berlin: Jovis, 2013); and Francesca Ferguson and Urban Drift Projects, eds., ***Make_ Shift City: Renegotiating the Urban Commons / Die Neuverhandlung des Urbanen*** (Berlin: Jovis, 2014).

6 Nina Gribat, Hannes Langguth, and Mario Schulze, "'Make City' in Times of an 'Absolute Present': Exploring Alternative Urban Practices at Ostkreuz, Berlin," ***sub\urban*** 3, no. 3 (2015): 111-24.

7 Richard Florida, ***The Rise of the Creative Class*** (New York: Basic Books, 2002).

8 Erik Swyngedouw, "Governance Innovation and the Citizen: The Janus Face of Governance-beyond-the-State," ***Urban Studies*** 42, no. 11 (2005): 1991-2006.

9 Ulrich Brinkmann, Klaus Dörre, Silke Röbenack, Klaus Kraemer, and Frederic Speidel, ***Prekäre Arbeit: Ursachen, Ausmaß, soziale Folgen und subjektive Verarbeitungsformen unsicherer Beschäftigungsverhältnisse*** (Bonn: Friedrich-Ebert-Stiftung, 2006).

10 Sharon Zukin, ***Naked City: The Death and Life of Authentic Urban Places*** (Oxford: Oxford University Press, 2010).

11 Swyngedouw, "Governance Innovation and the Citizen: The Janus Face of Governance-beyond-the-State," (see note 8).

"The new nervous disorders of aesthetic capitalism are thus an expression of the economic necessity of and sociocultural desire for working in the home against the background of the new housing question."

The Uncertainty of Housing *Jesko Fezer* While intense local political struggles are being waged over the last remaining urban vacancies, the uncertainty once associated with them has long disappeared: Urban land serves the creation of economic value and should be valued as built-up space in terms of economic effectiveness. This certainty is producing new spaces of uncertainty: dwellings. Due to real estate profit-seeking or poor housing policies, dwellings are becoming either more expensive or worse in quality—or simply removed from the rental market.

Between 1903 and 1922 the Berlin Health Insurance Fund for Merchants, Traders and Apothecaries inspected the dwellings of its patients. Accompanied by officials from the health insurer, the firm of Heinrich Lichte photographed the interiors of 175 Berlin apartments. These images, reproduced as rotogravure prints with captions, were added in loose succession to the dwelling survey.[1] The aim of this annual report was to prove the long recognized connection between habitation and illness. The fact that the living conditions under scrutiny were also working conditions was only considered in passing.

It would be inappropriate to compare the misery described in these reports with the new housing shortage in the "start-up city" of Berlin. The hygiene detectives who, at the beginning of the last century, investigated and secured evidence of the causes of illness positioned individual pathologies within their sociospatial framework. However, now the afflictions of the present are also spilling out of the darkness of the private residential sphere. Users of affordable living space are becoming uncertain, not only because of the limited availability of this space and the threatened withdrawal of this resource, but also with regard to its socially promoted exploitation. Affordable living space is becoming not only a scarce commodity but at the same time a productive, economized sphere.

There seem to be many possibilities for dealing with the new housing question, the shortage of affordable living space. Rising rents could be offset by a reduction in the cost of living. Moving into a cheaper, smaller, less well located dwelling could also help as could the subletting of parts of larger dwellings or the temporary letting of living space as holiday housing. So-called alternative forms of habitation such as cohousing and shared dwellings counter the problem of rising costs with planned living-area reduction. Use optimization can also be achieved through the secondary use of dwellings as workplaces. Whether in the form of digital platforms for product retail, networked services, the possibility of flexible salaried employment, crowdworking or traditional working at home: in situations of significant economic pressure an attractive, socially established model of living and working is being located in the domestic sphere. Preferably from one's own bed: it seems that a desire for the intimacy of self-determined work has been awakened. And while the creative city generates the spatial, social framework for this form of self-economization, design as a discipline forms the guiding principle; as a promise, the horizon; and as a form-giver, the artifacts of this regime of self-determined work.

The diagnosed reactions to the ubiquitous demands of the creativity dispositif are exhaustion, depression, and attention-deficit disorders. These pathologies, the widespread incidence of which is a relatively new phenomenon, originate from the excessive demands made on the self by the perpetually creative subject, the associated craving for social recognition, and a self-esteem based on the potential for creative-economic action. Failure in the professional sphere due to a lack of flexibility, creativity, individual initiative, and passion promotes the prolific incidence of depression, a sense of inner emptiness, feelings of inferiority, and resultant lethargy. In new and unexpected ways, the social demand for consistent, productive activity is becoming located in private space, where it intersects with the uncertainty of economic-spatial conditions. The new nervous disorders of aesthetic capitalism are thus an expression of the economic necessity of and sociocultural desire for working in the home against the background of the new housing question.

1 See Gesine Asmus, ed., *Hinterhof, Keller und Mansarde: Einblicke in Berliner Wohnungselend 1901–1920* (Reinbek: Rowohlt, 1982).

B.—NE
Keibelstraße 34
Side wing, fourth floor

The apartment consists of a parlor and kitchen. The front part of the space, which serves as a living room, bedroom and work-room. The man makes wallets. The woman, who suffers from neurasthenia, helps as much as she can.

Shanghai
Paris
Sydney
Tokyo
London
Beijing
Seoul
Dubai
MAKE THE MOST OUT OF
YOUR SPACE
WWW.BOCONCEPT.COM
2017

B.—NE
Heinersdorfer Straße 13
Third floor

1911
1954
*

The patient is 75 years old and works as a hand weaver in his parlor, which also serves as his bedroom. Room dimensions: 5 m long, 5 m wide, 2.8 m high.

133

B.—N
Rheinsberger Straße 62
Basement

The apartment consists of a parlor and kitchen. The woman makes felt slippers and has to work by the window because the rest of the parlor is too dark. Two beds are available for five persons. The entrance to the apartment is dark, the stairs dirty.

1906
*
↓

82

Die Gestalt der Arbeit hat sich im 21. Jahrhundert grundlegend verändert. Oftmals müssen wir unser Haus nicht mehr verlassen, um einer Beschäftigung nachzugehen. Das Zuhause ist nicht mehr nur Ort des Rückzuges und der Familie, sondern hat sich dank elektronischer Vernetzung in einen voll ausgestatteten Arbeitsplatz verwandelt. Das erlaubt die Ausübung vieler Berufe inmitten der angenehmen Umgebung selbst gestalteten Lebens.

Wir können mit Hilfe von mobilen Computern und Telefonen fast überall auf der Welt miteinander kommunizieren. Selbst das Bildtelefon, als Gadget einst Helden in Science-Fiction Filmen vorbehalten, ist Wirklichkeit geworden. Und das Internet ermöglicht es, enorme Mengen an Daten in Sekunden vom einen Ende der Erde ans andere zu verschicken. So können wir Projekte verwirklichen, deren Mitarbeiter auf verschiedenen Kontinenten sitzen und sich vor den Bildschirmen ihrer Laptops zu Videokonferenzen versammeln, um zu diskutieren und Entscheidungen zu fällen.

Das klassische Ensemble des Büros, der Stuhl, mit dem man sich an den Tisch zur Arbeit setzt, gestaltet eine Verbindung von zwei Orten, die noch eine Generation vor uns nur getrennt kannte: Aus Home und Office wird Home Office.

Die Kollektion im Überblick: Home Office.

B.—NW
Wilhelmshavener Straße 27
Front building, ground floor

The apartment consists of a parlor and kitchen. The parlor serves as a workshop, shop and bedroom for one person.

Soft Edg

Soft Edge by Iskos-Berlin is a deeply resolv piece of design, made possible by a harmonic intersection between designer, technology ar manufacturer. Created in the knowledge tha there is no ultimate sitting posture, but rath that our natural state is one of constant dynamic movement creating a new level of comfort and aesthetic lightness.

B.—SW
Kreuzbergstraße 49

A kitchen that also serves as a workroom for the production of cigars. The children also contribute to the work. The wife is currently ill. Room dimensions: 3.7 m long, 2.6 m wide, 3 m high.

with other art world power brokers, but he isn't one for bourgeois comforts. Instead he approached his summer getaway as a project space, choosing a rundown residence in Rockaway Beach, an economically depressed urban beach town 20 miles from Manhattan that made headlines after being devastated by Hurricane Sandy (which hit just six months after Biesenbach moved in). The desperate situation (electricity, transportation, and water were not restored until months after the storm) immediately snapped Biesenbach into action, drawing on his organisational skills and activating his network of artists and celebrities towards an unexpected venture: an impressive, effective, and necessary year-long volunteer relief effort. As Biesenbach gives me a tour of his summer home he explains what was accomplished in Sandy's aftermath and why Joseph Beuys is incredibly important to him. I'm surprised to learn that, after art, the curator's next top priorities are plants and birds.

apartamento - the Rockaways

B.—SE
Manteuffelstraße 64

In this kitchen the mother makes Christmas crackers. The two school-aged children have to help her. Our 16-year-old female patient, who suffers from lung disease, sleeps in this room. Room dimensions: 4 m long, 2.75 m wide, 2.5 m high.

1911 ✱

124

Kaari Collection
Ronan & Erwan Bouroullec 2015
REB 005 Desk
artek

B.—E
Liebigstraße 25
Rear wing, third floor

The woman sews gym bags that she has designed herself to sell online. She occasionally works for film productions. She sleeps in the adjoining room with her 14-year-old daughter.

II. IMAGES

01 Alexanderplatz

02 Alexanderplatz

03 Dircksenstraße

04 Dircksenstraße / Voltairestraße

05 Monbijoupark

06 Mauerstreifen Sebastianstraße

07 Mauerstreifen Sebastianstraße

08 Tachelesgelände Oranienburger Straße

09 Bahnhof Friedrichstraße

10 Bahnhof Friedrichstraße

11 Spreeufer Michaelkirchstraße

12 Mauerstreifen Heinrich-Heine-Straße

13 Spreeufer Michaelkirchstraße

14 Mauerstreifen Heinrich-Heine-Straße

15 Jerusalemer Straße

16 Markgrafenstraße / Schützenstraße

17 Krausenstraße / Jerusalemer Straße

18 Mauerstreifen Heinrich-Heine-Straße

19 Alfred-Döblin-Platz

20 Bethaniendamm, "Baumhaus an der Mauer"

21 Friedrichstraße / Puttkamerstraße

22 Leipziger Straße, formerly Tresor club

23 Leipziger Straße, "Mall of Berlin"

24 Mühlenstraße, "East Side Gallery"

25 Mühlenstraße, "East Side Gallery"

26 Mauerpark

27 Cuvrystraße / Spreeufer

28 Gleisdreieck

29 Revaler Straße / Dirschauerstraße

30 In front of „Schlesisches Tor"

31 Lohmühlenstraße / Kiefholzstraße

32 Gleisdreieckpark / Yorckstraße

33 Tempelhof Airfield / Schillerkiez

26
02
01
03
04
11
13
06
07
12
14
18
17
15
19
20
24
25
29
27
30
31
33

plate 01

U
Alexanderplatz
ÜNDLICH BIS ZU

plate 02

EINSTEIN KAFFEE
EINSTEIN KAFFEE
Perfect

plate 03

Benediktiner
Weissbier
YAKUZA
CAFÉ • RESTAURANT
POMMES
CURRYWURST

plate 04

ALEXA
www.bigbike
Berlin an
WIR SUCHEN FAHRER-GUIDES
Call +49
(0)179 - 50 67 325
bigbike-berlin.de

plate 05

plate 06

plate 07

plate 08

ZEPPELIN
hier mieten!

plate 09

The Monki World
Friedrichstraße
Tränenpalast

plate 10

plate 11

plate 12

LIDL

plate 13

plate 14

plate 15

ab 01.06.16
06h
P
GESTE
Gesellschaft für Transport
und Entsorgung mbH
030 / 80 96 18 89
www.geste-gmbh.de
10097D
ZEPPELIN
hier mieten!

plate 16

Markgrafenstraße
Gehweg-
schäden

plate 17

98 - 333
NIEMEIER
MIETSTATION

plate 18

plate 19

plate 20

Friedrichstraße
Puttkamerstraße
Berliner Kindl
Berliner Kindl
IMBISS
CAFE

plate 21

Coca-Cola
Friedrichstraße
Puttkamerstraße
Der Spiel macher
Der Spiel macher
HOME & GARDEN
DAS ORIGINAL
30.6.–3.7.
30%
Neueröffnung
Checkpoint Charlie
Sadhguru
in Berlin
“In is the only way out”

plate 22

plate 23

SATURN
KAISER'S
SATURN
M·A·C
MALL OF BERLIN
M·A·C

plate 24

Geschützte Grünanlage
Berliner Mauer

plate 25

Mercedes-Benz Arena

plate 26

plate 27

plate 28

plate 29

plate 30

plate 31

plate 32

plate 33

Wachsende Stadt
richtig investieren
DIE LINKE.

Postscript *Markus Miessen* A generic city hall; the audience has been seated, still engaged in light conversation with one another: money talks. The mumbling is silenced by an official-looking gentleman who steps up to the microphone: he is a He, and aware of it, dressed in a slim-cut suit and a tie that seems just a bit too colorful. He dives immediately into the subject, the neighborhood city—a city that is codesigned and appropriated by its residents, so he says. He chooses his words carefully: he says "coauthors." He presents colorful renderings of urban squares with lush greenery and slick aluminum facades, kids playing with abandon, dogs off their leashes, young families who apparently know exactly what kind of city they want and need. The audience in the city hall is impressed and starts mumbling again, fascinated not only by the flawless images of a future without problems but also by the impeccable verbal presentation interspersed with humor at just the right moments. Our man dwells on the potential of inclusion, open frameworks, and the liberation of the citizen. Just before another figure is introduced onto the stage, he says his two final sentences, his voice raised slightly more than necessary: "This project will not only bring new investment to this area, it will give people the opportunity to finally feel at home, to participate in what will be their city. And this is the man who will help us turn this vision into reality!" The architect takes over the microphone.

Concept: Kenny Cupers and Markus Miessen
Texts by individual authors
Photographs 2001: Kenny Cupers and Markus Miessen
Photographs 2016: Kenny Cupers and Thomas Schirmer

Translation from German into English: Joseph O'Donnell
Copy editing: Keonaona Peterson
Project management: Alexander Felix, Regina Herr
Production: Heike Strempel
Design: Lena Mahr

Paper: Munken Print White, 1.5, 100 g/m^2 and 150 g/m^2
Printing: Grafisches Centrum Cuno GmbH & Co. KG, Calbe
Lithography: [bildpunkt] Druckvorstufen GmbH

Library of Congress Cataloging-in-Publication data
A CIP catalog record for this book has been applied for at the Library of Congress.

Bibliographic information published by the German National Library
The German National Library lists this publication in the Deutsche Nationalbibliografie; detailed bibliographic data are available on the Internet at http://dnb.dnb.de.

This publication is also available as an e-book (ISBN PDF 978-3-0356-1440-4) and in a German language edition (ISBN 978-3-0356-1438-1).

P.O. Box 44, 4009 Basel, Switzerland
Part of Walter de Gruyter GmbH, Berlin/Boston

Printed on acid-free paper produced from chlorine-free pulp. TCF ∞

Printed in Germany

ISBN 978-3-0356-1439-8

9 8 7 6 5 4 3 2 1 www.birkhauser.com